Faces of the Adversary

ABRAHAM ADESEYE

FACES OF THE ADVERSARY

A COMPLETE PORTRAIT OF THE ENEMY

Belleville, Ontario, Canada

Faces of the Adversary

National Library of Canada Cataloguing in Publication

Adeseye, Abraham, 1964-
    Faces of the adversary : a complete portrait of the enemy / Abraham Adeseye.
ISBN 1-55306-786-X.--ISBN 1-55306-788-6 (LSI ed.)

    1. Devil--Christianity. 2. Spiritual warfare--Biblical teaching. I. Title.

BT982.A44 2004   235.47   C2004-901762-4

For more information, please contact:
Adebayo Abiodun Adeseye
33 Cecil Avenue, Barking, Essex, UK, IG11 9TD

Guardian Books is an imprint of *Essence Publishing,* a Christian Book Publisher dedicated to furthering the work of Christ through the written word. For more information, contact: 20 Hanna Court Belleville, Ontario, Canada K8P 5J2. Phone: 1-800-238-6376. Fax: (613) 962-3055. E-mail: publishing@essencegroup.com Internet: www.essencegroup.com

Table of Contents

Note to Readers

If you would like to enquire further about issues raised in this book or if you feel that the author could be of help, you are invited to write to him at 33 Cecil Avenue, Barking, Essex IG11 9TD, UK, or telephone 44 (0) 208 491 5858, or email Pastor@mightyrock.org.uk

It may also be of interest to know that the author normally ministers at Mighty Rock Assembly, London, UK on Sundays from 11 a.m. to 1 p.m. and Thursdays from 7 p.m. to 9 p.m. We are an interdenominational charismatic church. An open invitation is extended to all and particularly to those interested in deliverance and related themes. Details of service venue will be provided on enquiry. They are also available on our Web site: www.mightyrock.org.uk.

Introduction

L ife is a battle. We have an enemy who does not want us to discover and enter into the fullness of God's will for our lives. God's will is the Garden of Eden. Satan's will is for man to live outside the garden, cut off like himself from God and all that is good. That, however, is not the full story.

The Bible makes it clear to us that Satan is a defeated foe. Colossians 2:15 says that Jesus disarmed principalities and powers and made a public spectacle of them, triumphing over them by the cross. John 12:31 says that Satan has been broken and his power over man destroyed in Christ. Jesus took away his power according to Hebrews 2:14, and all power now belongs to Christ according to Matthew 28:18. Therefore Satan's ability in your life is now limited to what you allow him to do. Your choices determine your life and Satan cannot control your choices. God says in Deuteronomy 30:15,19 that the choice is yours—life or death, prosperity or adversity, blessing or curse. The choice is yours. Man is no longer a victim of anything or anyone. It is now possible for man to fulfil the purpose for which God made man. He made man in his own image to rule over the works of his hands, says Genesis 1:26. He did all this to fulfil the purpose he has for man in Christ Jesus from all eternity (2 Timothy 1:9). Therefore, it is clear that man did not first enter God's mind in Genesis 1. God conceived of man from all eternity before the foundation of the world because of the great love he has for his son.

God is a family God. He loved his son so much he wanted more children. That is why you and I exist. That is the reason God made us—to be part of his household. However, unlike the Son, Jesus, who was not created but begotten, we are created and it is the nature of God as love that every created being must have a choice. Love dictates that God cannot force us to be his children. We must decide who our spiritual father is. People often complain that they had no choice about who their natural parents would be. Well, we have a choice about the more important one—our spiritual parentage. Man made the choice to follow Satan in Eden, and we can see the result all around us. However, as I said earlier, that is not the real story. It is only a distraction. The real story of man is the one contained in God's mind. God told us what this is in Genesis 1:26. Man is made for dominion, for glory, exaltation and honour. Moreover, God has not failed in any project he has embarked upon. In fact, it is the nature of God that he cannot fail. He says in Isaiah 46:10 that his purpose will be established and he will accomplish all his good pleasure. When he plans something, no one can frustrate it (Isaiah

14:27). Therefore, the plan God has for man is certain of fulfilment, and the plan God has for you personally is sure of fulfilment. It is up to you to choose whose plan you want to execute in your life—God's plan or Satan's plan.

The Deceiver

S atan is a deceiver. His main weapon before and since his defeat by Jesus Christ is deception. It is by deception that he got Eve to eat the forbidden fruit. He is a liar and the father of lies (John 8:44). Since God is truth, it follows that Satan can only operate through deception. His main strategy is to try to get man to think, believe, talk and act on his lies. There is no truth in him. The Bible says he is the deceiver of the whole world (Revelation 12:9). He has developed for 6,000 years a web of deceit to try to get man to miss his divine destiny. He fools man by hiding behind a complex web of deception. If things were exposed simply as being a duel between God and Satan, man will not be easily fooled as he is now.

The Battleground

Satan operates through camouflage. In Eden, he took the form of a serpent. He is still talking today though we may not see a serpent. He talks though the media, our peers, circumstances and emotions. His target is our minds. Since his defeat by Jesus, he can no longer take the believer on in the spiritual realm. He targets his lies at the mind. His tool is mental reasoning. He does not announce himself to you as a thief, liar and murderer. Instead, he and his demons use thoughts to try to get us out of God's will. The battleground is the mind, but you decide who wins— the Word of God, or Satan. The mind is the arena where you wrestle with evil spirits (2 Corinthians 10:5). Thoughts are the devil's weapons but 1 Corinthians 9:1 says no soldier serves as a soldier at his own expense. God in his grace has provided us with everything to win right now (2 Peter 1:3). He has given us spiritual as well as physical resources, strategy, wisdom, armour, weapons and leadership for victory. It is impossible for Satan to win.

The combination of the Word of God, the anointing of the Holy Spirit, the blood of Jesus, the love of the Father, together with the ministry of angels are an impenetrable and unyielding fortress against anything Satan and his cohorts have to offer. Therefore, he relies on you believing his lies instead. He works hard—very hard, trying to get you to think his own thoughts. Every time you think lustful thoughts, or thoughts of hate, anger, bitterness, vengeance, prejudice, worry, fear, anxiety, depression, hopelessness or gloom, you are thinking the thoughts of Satan. Every time you think negative thoughts about people or situations, you are thinking the devil's thoughts. He tries to get you to live inside your mind with the thoughts that he plants. As a man thinks, so he is. So the devil seeks to cut you off from the thought wrapped up in the Word of God—the word of truth, the life, abundance, health, peace, joy, success, greatness, victory and glory. He seeks to get you to focus on 'this present darkness' instead of 'this marvellous light', ' this present Jesus', 'this present Holy Spirit', 'this present victory', 'this present anointing' or 'these present angels'. Just as the venom of a poisonous snake enters a body and cuts off the blood circulation causing death, the enemy seeks to cut us off from the light, life and love of God by trying to get us to fill our minds with his lies, and reason with him.

We have no business reasoning with the enemy. He is not entitled to our attention. He does not deserve it. 2 Corinthians 10:5 says we must smash in pieces all arguments, reasoning, theories and imaginations that are contrary to the counsel of God and take captive every thought to the Word of God. The mind is the control centre for all actions, so the enemy seeks to get you to give him a place in your mind. You must never allow him to get into your thoughts. Once you suspect his lies in your mind, use the Word of God—the quick and active sword of the Spirit, to cast them down.

Pray like this:

In the mighty name of Jesus, I break down all strongholds of lies that the enemy has built in my mind. I cleanse my mind with the blood of Jesus. Amen.

Life is a battle. This world is full of evil spirits who are the foot soldiers of Satan and the principalities and powers in the heavenly places. They are in rebellion against God, and this earth is their temporary sphere of operation before they are finally destroyed in the lake of fire created for them (Matthew 25:41). They deceive, delude, seduce, tempt and seek to lead man astray. They have opted out of the goodness of God, and they are seeking to deceive multitudes to opt out of God and be condemned with them. They are wicked and evil in the extreme. There is no good in them. Their plans, purposes and modes of operation are likewise evil. Isaiah 32:7 says their weapons are evil and their schemes, wicked. Their primary tool in their agenda of subversions is lies. Their mission is to subvert the good purposes of God for man. However, as we noted earlier, God cannot fail and the battle is not lost. If there is any loss, it is theirs.

Before the foundation of the earth, God put in place a plan of redemption to deliver you and me from them— and we are delivered. Colossians 1:13-14 say we believers in Jesus Christ have been delivered from Satan's dominion and authority, the authority he stole from Adam. The authority was never his in the first place—he got it by default through deception. Nevertheless, Christ took it back for us. We have been translated to the kingdom of God where Satan has no authority whatsoever. He will not tell you this though. It is called bluffing. He is the master of the bluff and psychological games. He seeks to fool even elect but Jesus has promised that this is not possible as long as we listen to the voice of the Spirit of God within. The Spirit is our companion in this journey. He is the interpreter of the road map. He is the truth and will guide us into all truth. Satan cannot win if we listen to the Holy Spirit, our guide, comforter and helper. If you have never given your life to Jesus, you are under the authority of

Satan. God wants you out of there today (Acts 26:18). He wants you out of darkness.

Pray this prayer:

Father God, please forgive me my sins in the name of your Son, Jesus Christ. I accept Jesus Christ as my Lord and Saviour. I give my life to you, O God. Make me your child and give me your Holy Spirit. In Jesus' name. Amen.

If you pray this prayer and you mean it, you are now a child of God. You now have eternal life (1 John 5:13). God is now your Father and Jesus Christ is now your Lord and Saviour. Satan is defeated in your life. He cannot touch you anymore (1 John 5:18). All he can do now is tempt and accuse you. However, he is a loser—one that will not go away and stop hassling. You are now a threat to his kingdom. You are now a beacon of light to dispel darkness in this world. You are now part of God's army of liberation. You have Jesus as your Commander and the angels as your protectors. The Holy Spirit is now living in you. You are now covered with the blood of Jesus and you have ambassadorial authority to use his name to advance his kingdom. You are now Satan's real enemy. You can now hit Satan where it hurts—you can now damage his interests. You are now a threat to his agenda. His fiefdom is more vulnerable now. Heaven is full of joy at your salvation, and the plan of God for your life is sure of fulfilment. Welcome to the family.

The first thing you need now is a new mind. Like a computer, your mind had been running on some programmes, but they were the wrong ones—the enemy's own.

You now need to renew your mind—to install new programmes in it—God's programmes, the Word of God. Romans 12:2 says we are to be transformed by the renewing of our mind because it is only with this new mind that the good, acceptable and perfect will of God for our life will be discovered and accomplished. Ephesians 4:22 says that the old programme of the devil was a programme of deception and corruption. The lies of Satan, when they are believed and acted upon, lead only to one thing—ruin. Galatians 6:8 says whoever sows to the Spirit shall, from the Spirit, reap eternal life. Eternal life is the will of God for us—eternal life in quality and quantity, and it starts now. It is a life of righteousness, peace and joy in the Holy Spirit. A life of success and inner fulfilment; a life of abundance of every good thing. Jesus says he came that we may have life in abundance, to the full, until it overflows. To have this life and enjoy it, Ephesians 4:2-4 says we need to be renewed in the spirit of our mind and put on the new self, which in the likeness of God has been created in righteousness, holiness and truth. In other words, we need to begin to function like God, in thought, speech and action, no less. That is the kind of exalted idea God had in mind when he made us. We need to begin to think, believe, speak and act upon his Word. The Word of God expresses the thoughts of God, and it is in it that we will find the answer to all our needs.

In fact, that is why God wrote it in the first place, and that is why the enemy tries to get man to marginalise it. However, 2 Timothy 2:9 says the Word of God cannot be bound. History proves that to be true. The devil is not going to beat God at anything—ever. The Word of God is Spirit and it gives life when it is believed and acted upon.

It is the power of God (see Romans 1:16, 1 Corinthians 1:18, 1 Thessalonians 2:13). This Word of the Spirit is our road map to success and fulfilment, and the Holy Spirit, its author, is the interpreter of the map for us. Therefore, we need a new mind—a spiritual mind, a mind that thinks spiritual thoughts and originates spiritual words, all having their source in the Spirit of God (1 Corinthians 2:13). It is the living and active Word of God that will erase all the lies of the enemy from our mind and make us who God wants us to be.

Pray this prayer:

Holy Spirit, create in me a new heart and mind, and renew a right spirit within me. In Jesus' name. Amen.

Garden of Eden

In the Garden of Eden, we see the enemy as a crafty, evil, low-down, no-good, cheating, hypocritical, filthy, perverted, lying rip-off artist. We see him as an ignoble, unjust, impure, ugly, sinful, bad and condemnable liar. He has not changed. His methods haven't changed, and his intentions remain the same. Jesus told us what these are in John 10:10. The thief comes only to steal and kill and destroy. He is ultimately responsible for all the evil in the world, and God in his justice has decided that there will be no forgiveness for him and his demons. Man, whom he fooled in the garden, was immediately promised redemption and Jesus came to accomplish it for us.

In the garden, we see the liar appearing for the first time on the pages of history to do his evil work. He had led a rebellion against God in heaven, and had been expelled from there. He was once an angel called Lucifer. In love with his own beauty, he fell into pride and selfishness. His rebellion manifests in five 'I will' statements addressed against God in Isaiah 14:13-14. In five utterances, he declared that he will take the place of God, etc., but God answered him with five responses in verses 15-20. Satan will be thrown down into hell; be gazed upon, that is, made a spectacle of; be talked about, mocked and scorned; be cast out like a carcass; and be alone. Satan's rebellion happened prior to Genesis 3, but in Genesis 3, we see him appear to do his evil work which he is still doing today.

He approached Eve. The cunning thief knew better than to approach Adam. He approached Eve. He still does that today. He is a subversive and he works by trying to subvert those in authority. The Bible says that man is the head of the woman. The devil knew this. Today, in his work against God and man, he works by subverting authority and order. He tries to get man to rebel against God's authority, to get woman to rebel against man and children to rebel against their parents. Where there is order, he cannot do his work, so the first thing he tries to create is disorder, disharmony, disunity, resentment, dissatisfaction, and ultimately, rebellion. He is the architect of pandemonium and confusion. He launches his attack against anything representing order, for God is a God of order. The family is the foremost symbol of order in society, and the enemy has concentrated his evil on the family. Fifty years ago, society was coherent because families stayed together. Today, the onslaught of the enemy against the family has resulted in high divorce rate, abortion on demand, homosexuality, child delinquency, family breakdown and dysfunction. These are just a few examples of crimes perpetrated by the enemy against mankind for which he will suffer eternally.

Eve's foremost mistake was to enter into a conversation with the enemy. The enemy wants to talk to Christians who allow him to do so. We have nothing to say to the enemy. What does any right-thinking person have to say to a lunatic like Satan? Nothing, if one is in one's right mind. Genesis 3:1 says the devil spoke to the woman and she responded. What a mistake. Never enter into a conversation with the liar. A child of God only has words of truth to speak, and Satan is never a suitable being to converse with. If you ever say anything to him, let them be words of rebuke as Jesus did in Matthew 16:23. The Bible says the mouth of the wicked pours out evil things. Satan only has evil things to say, and they are not the sort of things a child of God needs to hear. He will talk to you though. Once you become a child of God, he makes you a target of his poison. Psalm 5:9 says there is nothing true or reliable in whatever Satan or his demons say. Their inward part is destruction, their throat an open grave. Psalms 58:4 and 140:3 tell us that Satan's words are poisonous, and he wants to speak them to you constantly.

In Revelations 16:13, demons are compared to frogs. One thing about frogs is that they never keep quiet. Noise is their chief characteristic. So the enemy wants to speak his poison to your mind continuously. He likes spitting his venom at the believer, and he expects you to argue reason and converse with him. He wants his lies to be heard, listened to, meditated upon and responded to constantly.

21

Well, this is archetypal evil and must never be done. It is part of the strategy of wearing down the saints mentioned by Daniel. Eve entertained the enemy. Make sure you do not repeat her mistake. The Bible says there are many voices in this world uttering the words of the enemy. Deny them your attention. Do not even acknowledge him. Ignore him and get on with working out of your salvation. He has no contribution to make to your destiny. He is your enemy. Never trust your enemy. Never trust your enemy to converse with, and Satan is the most deplorable enemy imaginable. The Bible says our conversation is with God, not with Satan. If he has anything to say about you, God's elect, let him say it to God and get the same answer from God that he got in Zechariah 3:2: *'The LORD rebuke you, Satan!'*

Whether it is threats he utters or smooth words, treat them alike. God said to Ezekiel in chapter 2:6 that the words of rebellious ones are not to be feared.

> *Neither fear them nor fear their words, though thistles and thorns are with you and you sit on scorpions; neither fear their words nor be dismayed at their presence, for they are a rebellious house.*

Satan and his cohorts are in rebellion against God. In fact, Ephesians 2:2 says Satan is the one at work in the rebellious people. He is their leader. He doesn't deserve to be feared. To fear and submit to the thief is to invite the wrath of God, the real authority. No one can serve two masters; you cannot fear God and fear Satan at the same time. So God commands us not to fear Satan. God told Jeremiah in chapters 1 and 15 that God's servants must never fear the enemy: *'Do not be dismayed before them, or I will dismay you before them'* (Jeremiah 1:17). God has made his servants a fortified city, pillar of iron and walls of bronze against the enemy. *'They will fight against you but will not overcome you, for I am with you to rescue and save you'* (Jeremiah 15:20, NIV). In Isaiah 8:11-14, the Lord told Isaiah with mighty power, and in the strongest terms, never to be afraid. *'Do not fear anything except the LORD Almighty. He alone is the Holy One. If you fear him, you need fear nothing else. 14He will keep you safe'* (Isaiah 8:13,14, NLT). So the enemy's threats are just that. He can do nothing: *'Like a scarecrow in a cucumber field are they... Do not fear them, For they can do no harm. Nor can they do any good'* (Jeremiah 10:5).

Satan functions by surprise. He never announces his attacks beforehand, so anything he says is a bluff. The Bible says he is a roaring lion. That is all he is—a roaring lion, a bluffing lion. A serious lion doesn't roar. A lion only roars when it is seeking to paralyse with fear. A lion in an advantageous position doesn't roar. It is always quiet. Satan is never quiet because he is looking for an advantage. The animal is looking to paralyse with fear. Never cave in to his threats. When he sees that threats don't work, he tries smooth words; it is smooth words that he used with Eve. He didn't threaten her. When he approaches you with smooth words, ignore him. John 8:44 says his intent is murderous and his weapon is deception. Deceitful words are the kisses of an enemy (Proverbs 27:6). So treat his smooth words like the plague. Daniel 11:32 says it is smooth words that the enemy uses to deceive the unsuspecting, and 2 Corinthians 11:2 says this is what the serpent did with Eve. God said to Jeremiah in chapter 12:6

that the enemy is a traitor. *'Do not believe them, Even though they speak smooth words to you'* (NKJV).*'*

Pray:

I refuse to entertain the devil in my life. I choose life, blessing and prosperity. I reject death, curse and adversity. In Jesus' name. Amen.

The chief aim of the enemy is to separate man from his maker, in thought, word and deed. He seeks to deceive man into excluding himself from the life of God. Revelations 4:11 says we are created for God's pleasure. The chief purpose of man is to know God and to enjoy him forever. That we may know him and the one whom he has sent is eternal life. Knowing God is life. To not know him is death. Satan chose death and misery for himself. He confessed with his own mouth in Job 1:7 that he goes to and fro, back and forth. I call that misery. There is no peace for the wicked. They are like the troubled sea. They cannot rest. Satan cannot rest. God rested from his work and Jesus is seated at the right hand of God, but Satan goes to and fro, back and forth. What misery.

The anointed cherub that covers the throne of God becomes a vagabond on earth—by choice. The son of the morning becomes the father of the night. The bearer of light becomes the prince of darkness! What tragedy. But that is his own problem. We know God, and we will serve him forever. Satan won't succeed in any way, shape or form in our life—that marauder, vagabond and thief of the night. We are not of the night but of the day. We are children of light, not of darkness.

Pray:

Let every operation of darkness against my life come to nothing. Amen.

So the liar approached Eve. God is unjust, God is unfair, he suggests. He gave you every tree, but how unfair of him to deny you this one tree. This one tree that will take your eyes off the tree of life, oneness, wholeness, holiness, harmony and peace. This one tree—of the knowledge of good and evil—that will forever introduce division into your consciousness: good and evil; rich and poor; health and sickness; marriage and divorce; fertility and barrenness; abundance and lack; angels and demons, etc. How unfair of God to try and spare you all this trouble by asking you to keep away from that tree. The liar is still saying the same today. God is unfair and unjust is the perennial accusation of the evil one and his dupes. If God is good, why is so and so happening, they say. If God is not good, such attacks and character assassination would meet with instant judgement. God is good and we are glad to declare it. In fact, he is the only one that is good, says Jesus. The enemy would like us to distrust God—the irreproachable, benevolent, ever-loving Father who is love. The enemy would like to be God. That is the greatest desire of his heart—crookedness and evil in the extreme. He tried and he failed. God will not be put under pressure by anyone.

So the sore loser goes about badmouthing God at ever opportunity. Hasn't he been saying the same to you? If God is good, why haven't you got twenty-five million dollars in the twenty-five years you've been working, and all such nonsense. The foul spirit accuses God to man and he accuses man to God. There is no truth in him. It is impossible for him to speak the truth. In England, we speak English. In France, they speak French. In hell, they speak lies. Jesus said that when Satan lies, he is speaking his natural language for he is a liar and the father of lies. The next time the devil comes to you with his 'if God is good' nonsense, tell him where to go. We must never entertain any accusations against God. Lust wasn't fatal to Eve, but the moment she doubted God, Satan had her. To distrust God, his word and his character is to open the way for the enemy to move in for the kill. Lift high your shield of faith, of unshakable trust and total reliance on the truth, goodness and faithfulness of God and his Word. When you do this, the enemy is forever beaten and disgraced, which is what the animal deserves.

So we see the liar in Genesis 3:4 now bold enough to state an outright lie. Once he had got Eve's attention and planted doubt in her mind concerning God, the enemy now went for the jugular, and directly contradicted God's Word. This is the way he functions. The enemy is a coward. Anyone who knows anything about him knows that. His dependence on lies is primary evidence of his cowardice, for the liar is never bold enough to operate in truth. Being a fearful creature at heart, he depends on lies to keep his dupes in line, lest they find out the truth and he loses his grip on them. The Bible talks about the enemy coming in like a flood in Isaiah 59:19, but anyone who knows Satan knows that his initial approach is always the form of a drip. It is only when his poisonous drips are entertained that he feels confident enough to come in like a flood. The lesson is this: never entertain the poisonous drips of the enemy. They pollute, they corrupt and eventually, they destroy, which is what the enemy is after. He felt bold enough to contradict God's Word, only after Eve had opened the door of her mind to him.

Pray:

Every seed of doubt that the enemy had planted in my mind, I uproot you with the sword of the Spirit in Jesus' name. Amen.

The Oppressor

TWO

Acts 10:38 tells us that apart from being a deceiver, Satan is an oppressor. Oppression is a chief characteristic of the wicked. The Bible says the wicked cannot sleep without committing wicked atrocities. He loves to oppress, Hosea 12:17 tells us of the enemy. And the very tool he uses in his evil work of oppression is deception. Cunning and deception are in his hands, says Hosea 12:7, and with these he does his work of oppression. Oppression and deceit do not depart from the wicked, says Psalm 55:11. Jesus went about doing good, setting free those who were oppressed of the devil. In Luke 4:18, Jesus declared his mission as one of liberation. He came to set free those who were under the oppressive yoke of the enemy. He came to release the captives and set free those who were in bondage to the enemy; and Acts 10:38 tells us that this is what he did. Psalm 56:1 tells us that the enemy fights all day long to oppress God's people. In his arrogance, the evil lunatic prides himself on oppression (Psalm 119:122). Our task, as God's people, is to resist him. We must not allow him to oppress us in any way. He fights indeed like a dragon. The dragon is the symbol pf the enemy's wickedness, just as the serpent is the symbol of his craftiness.

A dragon is also a serpent, but a very wicked one. Thus, we see that deception and oppression do indeed go together. The wicked one fights like a dragon to oppress daily, and all day long. That is the warfare of the saint. The Bible says we are to take up the full armour of God, so we may be able to resist the enemy and stand firm against his schemes. Three times in Ephesians 6:10-13, we are told to stand firm against the oppressor and his oppressive schemes, stratagems, wiles and devices. It is lies that he works with, and we are told to resist them. We are given five defensive pieces of armour and one offensive piece, plus prayer. The defense of the believer is of extreme importance and that is why we have been given so many defensive weapons. The enemy fights all day long to oppress. He hates a joyful Christian. We are to be fully armed against his evil missiles calculated to knock us out. 1 Peter 5:9 and James 4:7 say we should resist him, steadfast in our faith until he flees. We must never give him an opportunity to oppress us emotionally, mentally or physically (Ephesians 4:27). As we enforce God's royal will on earth, we must resist any attempt by Satan to oppress us—daily. 2 Corinthians 10:4-5 says we are to use our mighty weapons to destroy all of the devil's strategies.

A mighty fortress is our God, a bulwark never failing—never failing when the enemy is dealt with in his strength. Be strong in the Lord, and in the power of his might. 1 Chronicles 16:11 says we should be strong in the Lord continually to deal with the enemy. The continual strengthening of the Holy Spirit, our inner strengthener, helper, comforter and guide, ensures steady defeat for the enemy.

Pray like this:

In the mighty name of Jesus, I cast down every evil arrow of the enemy targeted against me. Amen.

Egypt

The battle for freedom started in Egypt—the world. Exodus 1:10-11 showed us the heart of the enemy. Let us deal shrewdly, he says to his demons, so that man will not realise who he is, and enter into his destiny. Let us oppress them and keep them in bondage so that they will not leave the dominion of darkness and join forces with God in the kingdom of his son, Satan's great enemy. Let us oppress them, he says, so that they may not join God's side in the cosmic conflict. The cruel tyrant, always motivated by fear of the good and the godly, seeks to use cruelty as a weapon of suppression. But God is not going to be beaten. All the enemy's efforts proved vain, for God is the strength of his people. It is only the person who can defeat God that can defeat God's people. Verse 12 says the more the enemy oppressed the people, the more the people flourished— and the enemy's fear increased. Oppression is evidence of insecurity and we see it in Satan's puppets all over the world today. The Bible says woe unto him who fights with his maker. Woe indeed is what God has prepared for Satan and his cohorts, and the plague judgements on Egypt fore-shadow Satan's final doom.

The gods of Egypt were shown to be defenseless against our God, just as Satan is today without armour, having been overpowered, stripped and plundered by our saviour (see Luke 11:22, Colossians 2:15). In Exodus 4, God sent three messages to his people in the face of oppression, as well as to the enemy. He told Moses to throw down his staff, his symbol of authority. It became a serpent and Moses fled. Then God told him to pick it up by the tail. Serpents are picked up by the neck to prevent attack, but God told Moses to pick it up by the tail so as to show God's people and their leaders that Satan's power is derived power—delegated power. He uses it only with permission. He is a dog on a leash and can only bark, not bite. Secondly, God told Moses in verses 6-7 to put his hand in his bosom. It turned leprous. He put it in his bosom again and it turned fresh. This is a powerful message to God's people and a strong warning to the enemy that the enemy can be destroyed by God, at will. He is under God's power and God can do away with him as, and when, God chooses. Finally, in verse 9, God demonstrated to the enemy that he will indeed be judged. Just as he filled the Nile with inno-cent blood, he himself will perish in the Nile with his hordes. This is exactly what happened. God's enemies will be judged. Isaiah 41:11 says those who war with God's people will perish and be as nothing. We shall seek them and not find them. There is coming a time when Satan will be long forgotten, just a blip in history. The Bible says in Ezekiel 28:19 that the devil will be no more—no more in existence, no more in memory. Gone forever, like a bad smell. Philippians 1:28 says we are not to be alarmed by the enemy, for he will be destroyed. 2 Thessalonians 1:6 says God will repay with affliction and eternal destruction those who afflict his people. The enemy's final destiny is recorded in Revelations 20:10, in a place of eternal torment and misery—just what he deserves. In fact, God says the reason he made Lucifer is to show his power and to proclaim his name throughout the world (Exodus 9:16). So God is in total control of our enemy. Jesus said he chose his disciples even though he knew one of them was of the devil. Devils are no surprise to God. He knows them from the beginning to the end.

Pray like this:

Let every devil in my life perish and be as nothing in the name of Jesus. Amen.

Bargaining

When the oppressor is faced with the overwhelming power of God, he attempts to negotiate. In his desperation to hold on to the façade of not being a nonentity, he attempts to negotiate with God's servants. But we all know him to be a nonentity. He lost his place in heaven, and Jesus cast him out of authority on earth in John 12:31. He has no place, no status and no claim on anything. The only place left for him is misery in hell. We must never enter into negotiation with the thief. He didn't make man. He didn't redeem man. He has no claim over man, just as a thief has no claim on anything. When he attempts to negotiate with us concerning anything, let us give him a kick in the teeth. He loves no one and is good to no one. He has nothing to offer except lies. He is the original thief.

In Exodus 8:25, after a series of divine bombardment of the enemy—with weapons of mass destruction, no less—we see the enemy's first attempt at negotiation. Someone has said that the only thing Satan understands is a big stick. After a series of humiliating plagues, he calls Moses and tells him to serve God in Egypt. This is contrary to God's instruction. God's instruction is to leave Egypt (Exodus 3:18). Unless one is born again, he or she cannot see the kingdom of God. The enemy's plan is to get people into vain religiosity, a form of godliness without the power of God (2 Timothy 3:5). The enemy is not against religion. He is against God. People can have as much religion as they like, as long as God is not in it—as long as it is not true spiritual worship. The enemy is only scared by spiritual people, not religious people. So he suggests to Moses, 'Be religious but don't be born again; stay in the world, stay in the darkness and follow useless ceremonies and rituals—carefully devised tales and inherited futility'. We must not allow the enemy to deceive us with crass negotiations. God says we must leave darkness and Satan. He doesn't ask us to be religious. The Word of God is our lamp. We must follow it and not the enemy's lies.

Then he suggests to Moses in Exodus 8:28 that Moses should not go far away from his domain. 'Don't go all out for God. Don't serve the Lord with all your heart, mind, soul and strength as stated in Deuteronomy 6:5 and Matthew 22:37. Don't trust God all the way as Proverbs 3:5 says. Don't acknowledge him in all your ways. Just a little bit will do. Don't go the second mile, a mile will do'. Let us tell the enemy to go to hell—his true place, when he tries to tell us how to serve our God.

Then he suggests in Exodus 10:11 that Moses go with the men and leave the families behind, so that he can get his dirty hands on them. 'Make it compulsory for your kids to go to college but make church optional. Leave your spouse at home when you're going to church. Only one needs to go since you're one flesh'. Lies, lies, lies. The enemy is after families. I know a minister's child who is out there in the world today. This person grew up with as much of the devil's stuff in their life, and we can all see the result today. You and your family are in this together. I cannot stress enough the importance of serving the Lord with your family. God created the family and the enemy hates it. We must never allow the enemy to get his evil hands on any member of our family.

Pray this prayer:

Any design of the enemy to divide my family in serving God, I destroy by the power of the blood of Jesus. Amen.

Lastly, in Exodus 10:24, the thief says if he can't stop one's freedom, can't quench one's fire, can get one's family, he wants one's finances. He isn't called a thief for nothing. 'Don't serve God with your money, tithes, offering etc', the thief says. But like Moses, we must say to him, *'Not a hoof shall be left behind'* (Exodus 10:26).

Pray:

In the name of Jesus, let every plot of the enemy against my finances be destroyed by fire. Amen.

There must be no negotiation or compromise with the enemy. The battle belongs to the Lord. God delivered his people and he will yet deliver (2 Corinthians 1:10). He will deliver us from every evil work (2 Timothy 4:18). The Lord made a mockery of the enemy (Exodus 10:2). The oppressor's back was broken. The Lord's people were set free. The enemy was plundered and finally destroyed. What a great testimony to the power of our God. Hallelujah to the Lamb! Let the heart of those who seek the Lord rejoice, for God is the strength of his people and he delights in breaking in pieces the oppressor (Psalm 72:4).

Pray:

Let all oppression of the enemy be crushed in pieces, in the mighty name of Jesus. Amen.

Health and Healing

One area that the enemy carries out his evil work of oppression is the area of health. There is a lot of deception in this area. Many have succumbed to the lies of the enemy and allowed the enemy to oppress them with sickness and infirmity. Sickness is a work of the devil. Jesus Christ is our healer. He is the health of his people. In Exodus 23:25, God promises to remove sickness from the midst of his people. In Deuteronomy 7:15, God says the same thing. The enemy's demons are agents by which he causes people to be sick. There are demons associated with all sorts of diseases. It doesn't serve God in any way for his children to be sick. Sickness is an evil thing. It has an evil source and its effect is evil. There is absolutely nothing consistent with God and godliness in being sick. God doesn't want you to be sick. The devil does. God has destroyed every spirit of infirmity that the devil has sent against me. God destroyed them with a vengeance, crushing and smashing them in pieces. Isaiah 53 says Jesus took away our sicknesses, diseases, sorrows and pains. Matthew, in chapter 8 of his gospel, verse 17, tells us that the atonement is the reason for healing. Healing is part of the atonement. Jesus healed and delivered everyone he met during his earthly ministry. Peter summed up Jesus' earthly ministry as one of healing and deliverance (Acts 10:38). Jesus said it is faith that heals people—faith in him and his Word.

By faith, two blind men were healed; the centurion's servant was healed; a dead girl was raised; a woman's bleeding stopped; Bartimaeus received his sight etc. Miracles didn't happen where there was no faith (Matthew 13:54-58). *'It shall be done to you according to your faith'*, Matthew 9:29 says. Jesus raised faith to the first place. He asked for it, commended it when he saw it, and attributed his healings to it. Faith is the key to your healing and deliverance. The law of faith is the highest law in the kingdom. We are saved by it, we are justified by it and we are blessed by it. We receive the Holy Spirit by it and miracles happen by it (Galatians 1-14). We must not let the enemy oppress us with ill health. Take Christ as your healer. He promises to renew our youth like the eagle (Psalm 103:5). Job 5:26 contains this wonderful promise: *'You will come to the grave in full vigor'*. Isn't this a promise of health, or don't we believe the Bible anymore? Have we reasoned away the Word of God in favour of the enemy's lies?

In Psalm 91, we are promised immunity from every disease imaginable. In fact, Deuteronomy 28 makes it clear that diseases are a curse, and Christ has redeemed us from the curse of the law (Galatians 3:13). Treat sickness like you treat the devil. It is of the devil. And don't listen to all the 'Paul had a thorn' stories—they are mere excuses that the enemy uses to get people into unbelief. The preponderance of biblical authority attest to sickness as being satanic. In John 3:14-15 Jesus himself used the incident of physical healing in numbers 21:8-9 as a type of his atoning work on our behalf. Physical healing and atonement cannot be separated. Believe and be healed!

Pray:

In the mighty name of Jesus, let every spirit of infirmity, weakness, sickness, illness, ailment, disease and disability be destroyed in my life by the blood of Jesus. I take Christ as my healer. He has redeemed me from all evil. I receive complete healing and full health, for by his stripes, I was healed. Amen.

The Darkness of Fear

The number one tool of oppression, control and manipulation that the enemy possesses is fear. Fear is darkness. To live in fear is to live in darkness. The Bible says God has delivered us from the domain of darkness and transferred us to the kingdom of his beloved Son (Colossians 1:13). Fear is to darkness what faith is to light. Without faith, it is impossible to please God; without fear it is impossible to please Satan. The Bible says we walk by faith, not by sight (2 Corinthians 5:7). The enemy needs fear—he is a thief. No legitimate, rightful, beloved person has need of fear. But a thief needs to put people in fear before he can steal. We have all seen bank robbers on television pull out a gun to rob the bank. The bank will not hand over its money to a robber ordinarily. But the robber uses fear, threats and intimidation to try to get people to hand him their possessions, their destiny, and other things. In the case of believers, whose eyes have been opened, and who have turned from the domain of Satan and darkness, he tries to oppress us with fear so as to steal our salvation and bring us back under his evil rule.

The Bible tells us in 1 John 4:18 that fear has torment. Isaiah 54:14 says in righteousness we shall be established; we shall be from oppression, for we shall not fear; and from terror, for it will not come near us. Terrorism is the deliberate use of fear to try to achieve an end. Without fear, the terrorist cannot operate. Isaiah 54:14 tells us that fear brings oppression. Fear oppresses the mind and brings chaos to it. 2 Timothy 1:7 says God has not given us a spirit of fear, but of power and love and a sound mind. Fear robs one of power. It distorts true love and brings chaos to the mind. If this isn't darkness, what is? The enemy seeks to agitate, trouble, cause inward commotion in, and disturb mentally with fear and perplexity, the believer, according to Galatians 1:7, for the sole purpose of doing his work of perversion and evil!

The Bible says we have not received a spirit of slavery and bondage leading to fear again, but we have received a spirit of adoption as sons by which we cry out, 'Abba! Father'. It was for freedom that Christ has set us free, no longer to be subject to a yoke of slavery. Paul says in

Galatians 2:5 that we must not yield to the enemy for even a moment, as he seeks to put us in bondage. Let him take his evil message elsewhere. We know better than to listen to the foul being. The Bible declares in Isaiah 32:5-6 that Satan is a rogue who goes about speaking evil nonsense. He seeks to get people to think and to believe what is wrong and evil about themselves, their life, relatives, future, etc. The Bible says in Proverbs 15:15 that all the days of the afflicted are made evil by fear. Proverbs 15: 4,13 says paying attention and meditating on Satan's perversion causes sadness and crushes the spirit. That is the main purpose of his lies. The joy of the Lord is our strength and Satan wants to steal our joy and our strength by working to get us to believe his fearful lies. Fear leads to worry and anxiety; anxiety produces depression (Proverbs 12:25) and depression leads to physical illness (Proverbs 17:22 and 18:14). So we can see that fear is a terrible thing. That is why the enemy operates in it.

Fear is the result of wrong believing. I call it 'bad' faith. God tells us not to listen to the rogue and his wicked lies. Isaiah 32:17 says this is what we are to think and believe: the work of righteousness shall be peace, and the effect of righteousness shall be quietness, confident security and assurance forever. *'My people will live in a peaceful habitation'*, says verse 18. *'You will keep him in perfect peace, Whose mind is stayed on You, Because he trusts in You'* (Isaiah 26:3, NKJV). *'Trust in the LORD forever, For in GOD the LORD, we have an everlasting Rock'* (Isaiah 26:4). He has disgraced our enemy. He has made him as ashes under the soles of our feet to trample upon (Isaiah 26:5-6, Malachi 4:3, Luke 10:19, Psalm 91:13, Mark 16:18). We have nothing to fear.

Isaiah 25:3-4 says God is our keeper, and if the enemy tries to mess with us, God will smash him. *'Should someone give Me briars and thorns in battle, Then I would step on them, I would burn them completely'*. Satan is no match for God. Isaiah 28:16 says Christ is our tried, tested and sure foundation. No one who believes in him will ever be ashamed, dismayed or disappointed. Isaiah 30:15 says in quietness and trust is our strength, not in fear and panic. God promises to protect his people in Isaiah 31:15. He is the stability of our times (Isaiah 33:6), a wealth of salvation, wisdom and knowledge. To fear him is enough. Isaiah 33:16 says our God is an impregnable Rock. Shame to the enemy forever!

God absolutely commands us not to fear. What is there to fear when God is your Father? The command not to fear runs throughout the Bible. It is sin of course (Romans 14:23). God said to Abraham in Genesis 15:1, *'Do not be afraid, Abram. I am your shield'* (NIV). Psalm 18 tells us that God is our Rock, fortress, deliverer, shield, salvation, stronghold and refuge. *'The name of LORD is a strong tower'* (Proverbs 18:10). Proverbs 30:5 tells us God is a shield to those who take refuge in him. If we trust the Lord, he will keep us safe (Proverbs 29:25). The fear of the Lord leads to life; then one rests content, untouched by trouble (Proverbs 19:29). *'No harm befalls the righteous, but the wicked have their fill of trouble'* (Proverbs 12:21, NIV). *'An evil man is trapped by his sinful talk, but a righteous man escapes trouble'* (Proverbs 12:13, NIV). Our God is a mighty fortress. His children will live in safety, and be at ease, without fear of harm (Proverbs 1:33). *'He guards the course of the just and protects the way of his faithful ones'* (Proverbs 2:8, NIV). You will go on your way in safety, and your foot will not stumble. When you lie down, you will not be afraid. When you lie down, your sleep will be sweet. Have no sudden fear of disaster or the ruin that overtakes the wicked, for the Lord will be your confidence, and he will keep your foot from being snared.

God's children have nothing to fear. *'A man cannot be established through wickedness, but the righteous cannot be uprooted'* (Proverbs 12:3, NIV). When a man's ways are pleasing to the Lord, he compels, yes commands even his enemies to be at peace with him (Proverbs 16:7). Do not fear, rejoice and be glad. Do not fear. You are hidden with Christ in God (Colossians 3:3). Nothing can touch the person that God hides (see Job 5:19-27). He who walks uprightly walks securely and is kept safe (Proverbs 10:9; 28:18). God said to Isaac in Genesis 26:24, *'Do not be afraid, for I am with you'* (NIV). The presence of God is our guarantee against fear of anything. *'Be strong and courageous, do not be afraid or tremble at them, for the LORD your God is the one who goes with you. He will not fail you or forsake you'* (Deuteronomy 31:6). *'Have I not commanded you? Be strong and courageous! Do not tremble or be dismayed, for the LORD your God is with you wherever you go'* (Joshua 1:9). *'Do not fear, for I am with you; Do not anxiously look about you, for I am your God'* (Isaiah 41:10). *'Do not fear, for I have redeemed you; I have called you by name; you are Mine!'* (Isaiah 43:1). *'Never will I leave you; never will I forsake you'* (Hebrews 13:5, NIV). *'Peace I leave with you; My peace I give to you; not as the world gives do I give to you. Do not let your heart be troubled, nor let it be fearful'* (John 14:27).

The peace that the world gives is ephemeral, but the peace of God passes all understanding. It is forever.

'For this is like the days of Noah to Me.... the mountains

may be removed and the hills may shake, But My lov-ingkindness will not be removed from you, And My covenant of peace will not be shaken," Says the LORD' (Isaiah 54:9-10).

So we have absolutely no reason to fear anything. Jesus says in John 14:1, *'Do not let your heart be troubled; believe in God, believe also in Me'*. Faith in God, his goodness and his love will remove all fear. Perfect love casts out fear (1 John 4:18). When the enemy takes aim at a life, fear is one of the weapons he tries to use. Luke 1:72-75 promises us that we servants of God, his children, have nothing to fear. When the enemy presents to us the reasons to believe what is wrong and be afraid—he operates through demonic logic—simply enter into God's rest. Don't reasoning with the devil. He is insane, and is trying to spread insanity across the world. We have already seen that fear is insanity (2 Timothy 1:7). A well mind, a whole, healed, sound mind doesn't operate in fear. We must not connect ourselves to Satan through fear. This is what Job did as he himself stated in Job 3:25-26. Sadly, Job was expecting trouble instead of peace, and the enemy moved in. He could never bring himself to rest quietly in the Lord. He offered sacrifices of fear continuously (Job 1:5). It wasn't long before the enemy moved in. Faith connects us to God; fear links us to the devil, to his mind, and his world of darkness. Come out of the darkness today.

Pray:

In the name of Jesus, I rebuke every spirit of fear trying to put me in bondage to the enemy. I enter into the light, life and love of Christ. Amen.

Fear is at the root of many evils—anger, worry, anxiety, jealousy, greed, disease etc. Faith, however, brings joy, peace, hope and power (Romans 15:13). Fear is a learned response to something that we don't understand, or is beyond our immediate control, or is out of control. To deal with fear other than by restful trust in God and his Word can be maintenance—intensive, for the enemy will constantly manoeuvre people or circumstances to disturb the person and trigger fear. We are called to overcome fear, not to manage it. If one's heart is steadfast in the love of God, it will be difficult for the enemy to disturb one's peace. Fear results from entertaining evil information and imagery, that is, information and imagery from an evil source—Satan, demons and their operatives. The devil constantly seeks to create terror in the mind by unleashing tyrannical, aggressive, oppressive and fearful thoughts so as to cause great suffering and torment. We must resist the enemy and make a firm decision. We must cast out his lies from our minds and fill our minds with true, noble, just, pure, lovely, attractive, virtuous and excellent thoughts from God's Word, as barriers to prevent the inflow of evil information and images from external sources.

When people fear, it is because the enemy is at work. Fear is faith in the devil and his lies. We must have only one source of information—God. Fear is the opposite of love (2 Timothy 1:7, Romans 8:15, 1 John 4:18). To fear is to deny God. As we grow in our understanding of God's love, fatherhood and care, we are able to cast away and overcome fear.

Pray:

Father, fill my heart with your love, in the name of Jesus. Amen.

Love brings calm and certainty while fear is an instrument of torment. We are not dependent on ourselves and are not totally responsible for our well-being, as God's children. So quit fearing and start trusting. The Bible says the mind set on the flesh, the senses, reason, appearance and circumstances is misery and trouble but the mind set on the Holy Spirit is life and peace (Romans 8:6). The enemy wants us to set our mind on his lies instead of God's truth. He wants us to absorb everything around us and become subjective, instead of believing God's Word. Thus, he is able to put people into bondage to fear of death, disease, difficulty, lack, the unknown, failure, the future, loneliness, criticism, rejection, loss of reputation, etc. But the Word of God doesn't promise evil for the child of God. He has promised good concerning us (Numbers 10:29). All we need is to trust him. Jesus came to set free those, through fear, were subject to slavery all their lives (Hebrews 2:15). Be free today! Stop fear and believe (Luke 8:50). We are God's champions. We are God's heroes, and like David before Goliath, we are called to be fearless.

Pray:

I declare myself free of every form of fear. I refuse to fear. In Jesus' name. Amen.

The Thief

THREE

O ne of the enemy's works on earth is poverty. It has been estimated that there are enough resources in the world for everybody to have fifteen million dollars each. But what do we see? Extreme wealth and poverty; abundance and lack; plenty and starvation. Let me make it crystal clear that this is not God's will for man. God made the Garden of Eden for Adam and Eve. Eden alone was fed by four rivers (Genesis 2:10-14). Gold, bdellium and onyx were there; God gave Adam and Eve dominion over everything he created. He gave man everything he created to use for their benefit (Genesis 1:26-29). From the names and description of the location of the four rivers, the area of Eden itself is as wide as the area promised to Abraham in Genesis 15:18-21. That was Adam and Eve's home region, their immediate vicinity. What abundance and generosity!

Our God is a generous God. He is a God of abundance. When he made water, he made oceans full of it. When he made air, he filled the whole atmosphere with it. He is a lavish God. He is a God of more than enough. Poverty, lack, penury, etc. do not enter into his thoughts for man. He is a God of exceeding abundance (Ephesians 3:20). God's plans for you are bigger than you could ever imagine. The Bible says eyes have not seen and ears have not heard, nor has it entered into the mind of man, the things which God has prepared for those who love him (1 Corinthians 2:9). God's plans for your life surpass even your wildest imagination. They are bigger than your mind can conceive. God's willingness to give is greater than your willingness to receive. He is not a mean, stingy God, reluctant to bless and needing persuasion. He made us because of a holy purpose in his mind requiring our existence (2 Timothy 1:9). Holiness means wholeness. Genesis 24:1 tells us that the blessing of Abraham that have come to us through Christ (Galatians 3:14) are blessings in EVERY way, not partial blessings.

Every child of God is entitled to believe God for the fulfilment of every promise of God in their life. That is what holiness, wholeness and blessing in every way mean. There is no poverty in the thoughts of God. 'I know the thoughts I think towards you, thoughts of blessing, joy, peace, abundance, success, victory, exaltation, honour and glory. Thoughts to give you the future you want, not one you don't want' (Jeremiah 29:11). There is a great future for a child of God (Psalm 37:37). God is our peace, Jehovah—Shalom. That word, peace, includes every blessing you can ever think of. Different versions of the Bible translate it differently for it is all-encompassing. Some translate it as peace. Others use prosperity, well-being, health, etc. It includes everything we could ever need for a successful inner and outer life. It is inward and outward fulfilment. Our God is a God of abundance. He has blessed us with every spiritual blessing in the heavenly places in Christ Jesus (Ephesians 1:3). You say those are spiritual blessings, not material. That is because you have accepted Greek philosophy.

All life is spiritual; heaven rules. It is impossible to gain the riches of heaven and not gain the riches of earth. *'But seek first His kingdom and His righteousness, and all these things will be added to you'* (Matthew 6:33), richly to enjoy (1 Timothy 6:11). In Deuteronomy 15:4, God says there should be no poor among you, for he will richly bless you. But in verse 11, God says there will always be poor people in the land, so help them. There *should* be no poor people, but there will always be poor people. I think that settles it. We have accepted what is as what should be. The fact that poverty exists doesn't mean it should exist or that God wants it to exist. Poverty is a curse, the result of poverty consciousness and thinking, poverty choices and practices. Anyone who believes in poverty will have poverty, for as a man thinks, so he is (Proverbs 23:7). When a person believes, speaks and practices poverty, that is what they get.

Choose, God says, prosperity or adversity, life or death, blessing or curse. It's your choice (Deuteronomy 30: 15,19). In Exodus 23: 25-31, Leviticus 26: 3-12, Deuteronomy 7:12-15 and Deuteronomy 28:2-14, every kind of prosperity and blessing is promised to the child of God, while poverty and adversity is promised to the enemies of God. *'Only the rebellious dwell in a parched land'* (Psalm 68:6).

Isaiah 1:19 says, *'If you consent and obey, You will eat the best of the land'*. Job 8:7 says, *'Your beginnings will seem humble, so prosperous will your future be'* (NIV). Job 22:21 says, *'Submit to God and be at peace with him; in this way prosperity will come to you'*. All the patriarchs were prosperous. Genesis 24:35 tells us that Abraham was very wealthy. Genesis 26:12-13 tell us that Isaac was wealthy, even reaping a statistic-bursting hundredfold harvest in one year. Jacob was not only rich, he actually received a prosperity plan to enable him to acquire wealth to fulfil his calling (Genesis 30:37-43; 31:9-13). God made him exceedingly prosperous, taking away Laban's wealth and giving it to Jacob. Doesn't the Bible say that wealth of the sinner is stored up for the righteous (Proverbs 13:22, Job 27:16-17; 20:15-22). Jacob suffered at the hands of Laban, and God transferred Laban's wealth to Jacob.

Pray:

O God, open my eyes today to your divine plan to make me rich. In Jesus' name. Amen.

The Bible says that we shall have the best of the land. I believe in the Bible from Genesis to the maps. This is no Old Testament stuff, as we shall see later. Haven't you been to the best part of town? Doesn't it challenge you that the heathens 'own' most of it? Did the devil create this world? Indeed, did the devil created anything? God has never relinquished ownership of this world and its contents, despite the devil's bogus claims. In Exodus 19:5, God says 'the whole earth is mine' (Leviticus 25:23). *'The earth is the LORD's, and the fulness thereof'* (Psalm 24:1,

KJV). The cattle on a thousand hills belong to him (Psalm 50:10). *'The silver is Mine and the gold is Mine'* (Haggai 2:8). Everything belongs to him (1 Chronicles 29:14-16). The devil owns nothing. So what entitles the devil's children to enjoy the best of our Father's properties? Didn't God tell us in Luke 15:11-32 that poverty belongs to the rebellious? The cause of poverty is estrangement from the Father. God shows us that when we come to him, we can expect the 'best' robe, a gold ring symbolising unlimited authority and right to the best things in life, sandals on our feet for our earthly journey, for underneath us are his everlasting arms, and to old age he carries us (Deuteronomy 32:11; 33:27, Exodus 19:4, Isaiah 46:4); and the fattened calf, which stands for life in its fullness and richness, not a dole of just the necessary ration. 'Let us eat and be merry,' the Father says to his people. In a land far away from God, poverty is to be expected, but with God, our only expectation should be the abundant life (John 10:10).

Pray:

I reject all thoughts of poverty and wrong beliefs I have acquired over the years, in Jesus' name. Amen.

Joseph, who had led God's people after Jacob, enjoyed the best of everything (Genesis 49:25-26, Deuteronomy 33:13-17). He is a type of Christ, of course, and the blessings Joseph enjoyed are what believers in Christ are entitled to enjoy. Joseph enjoyed prosperity and success in everything he did (Genesis 39:2,3,23). The people of God are promised abundance of all kinds—a life flowing with milk and honey, satisfaction and enjoyment (see Exodus

3:8,17; 13:5; 33:3. Leviticus 20:24, Deuteronomy 6:3,10,11;8:7-10;11:9-12; 26:9—all these repeat the promises). God says he gives his people the power to get wealth so as to establish his covenant (Deuteronomy 8:18). The people of God need wealth to do God's work. The Bible says we are to have, so that we will be able to give to our churches, the poor, missions, ministers, ministries, etc. How can we do any of these things if we are in poverty?

The Bible doesn't say wealth is for consumption. Wealth is for a purpose. 2 Corinthians 9:8-11 says God will enrich us with sufficiency in everything, and abundance for every good work. Titus 3:14 says we need to have, so that we can give to those in need. The good life is not just for ourselves to enjoy. It is also to do the necessary work of advancing the kingdom of God on earth and helping others. Poverty, I maintain, is a curse. It is foremost among the wicked works of the enemy. In Numbers 22:1-7, we see that the prosperity of God's people is a great threat to the enemy. Moab and Midian sought to have God's people cursed by Balaam, so as to bring adversity to Israel. But the four prophecies of Balaam in Numbers 23,24 concerning God's people, were of prosperity, success, victory, abundance, exaltation, honour and glory.

There was nothing anyone could do about it. No-one could curse those God had blessed—period. Then the enemy got to work. In Numbers 25, the plan was hatched to seduce God's people into idolatry, compromise and defeat. The Lord was angry against Israel. The enemy's tactics haven't changed. He needs people to squander their prosperity and blessing on sin. The people committed two evils. They forsook the Lord, the fountain of living waters, and made for themselves broken cisterns that could hold no water (Jeremiah 2:13). In a little time, they were impoverished. By the time of Gideon, we see in Judges 6 that the Midianite enemies that were threatened by Israel's prosperity in Numbers 22, but could do nothing about it, were now engaging in full scale economic terrorism against Israel, due to the latter's disobedience to God. Judges 1:1-6 tells us that the Midianites oppressed Israel economically, ravaging the land and destroying the crops. This resulted in the impoverishment of Israel. Satan is an economic terrorist and thief. He is wicked beyond imagination. His aim is to destroy the economic resources of God's people and impoverish them. The thief comes only to kill, steal and destroy (John 10:10).

Pray:

Every spirit of poverty operating against my prosperity, be shattered now by the blood of Jesus. Amen.

In fact, in 2 Kings 6:20-24 we see the enemy besieging Israel, resulting in poverty, famine and starvation. Poverty has always been the work of the enemy. Poverty doesn't exist in the mind of God. Satan is its architect. It is an instrument of oppression, as those affected by it know fully well. You must reject poverty, insufficiency or just getting by. Egypt was the land of not enough. The wilderness was the land of just enough. But Canaan is the land of more than enough. Luke 15:11-32, John 10:10 and 2 Corinthians 9:6-11 all say that your place is in the land of more than enough. The Bible shows us that God prospers his people. David gave billions of dollars in today's money for the building of the temple (1 Chronicles 29:2-5). Solomon is still the richest man ever to have lived since Adam and Eve, who theoretically were the richest couple ever since they possessed everything at one time. But Solomon was an uncommon achiever.

Solomon wasn't a perfect man, but he was a productive man. Jesus mentioned him a thousand years later in Matthew 6:29 and 12:42. He sought wisdom (1 Kings 3:7-9), and when he got it, he sought for more (Ecclesiastes 1:13). He pursued wisdom continuously, and he became very wealthy. People came from all over the world to exchange riches for his wisdom—kings and queens brought him their wealth because he was a wise man. He became very rich. Seek ye first the kingdom of God and his righteousness—his wisdom, power and Spirit, and all these things shall be added unto you. That was exactly what Solomon did. He asked God for his wisdom, Spirit and power to fulfil his divine destiny, and everything else was added unto him. *'A man's gift... brings him before great men'* (Proverbs 18:16), or as in Solomon's case, bring great men before him. A man skilled in his work will not remain in obscurity (Proverbs 22:29).

Money

What is money? Money is the symbol of God's abundance. It is a means of exchange, a part of day to day life. History and experience have shown that money is the result of earning it. God gives us power, ability, talents, gifts and ideas to get wealth. The law of wealth says give and it shall be given unto you (Luke 6:38). Money is a reward given in exchange for something of value. Never take anything without giving back more in value. Give love, friendship, encouragement, service, wisdom, etc. Give what you have, give back more in value than the money that you give or receive. This book is worth more in value than the money you paid for it. So bless me with your prayers. The Bible says it is more blessed to give than to receive because it is more productive. Everyone and everything gives, otherwise there would be no progress. The best thing you have to give will bring back the best thing you want to receive. According to the law of increase, giving leads to receiving and success brings success. Whoever has, to him shall be given, and he shall have abundance (Matthew 13:12). Jesus says it is only just for you to have what you have earned. He says your contribution to life, with what God has given you, determines what you get from life. If you don't use your talents, and you make no contribution, don't expect increase. I am not preaching self-reliance. I am only saying that God doesn't reward laziness. Where there is no reward for industry and effort, there would be no effort, progress would cease and society becomes extinct. God is a rewarder, and money is a reward. He only rewards faith and diligence (Hebrew 11:6). Christianity is not synonymous with laziness. I know ministers who work fourteen hours a day, and God rewards them. Woe to those who are at ease, declares Amos 6:1. I am not preaching self-reliance. Every child of God knows that we must trust God for the result of our efforts. We don't make it happen, God does.

Money therefore, comes in exchange for something of value that we give to those who need it. When we solve people problems and cater for their needs, money is given to us in exchange. It is as simple as that. When we give our best effort to the society, and we give our best to God, success comes. There is no reason for anyone to be poor. Those who are rich are rich because they know how to be rich. It has nothing to do with intelligence. Many intelligent people are poor, and many 'uneducated' people are rich. Prosperity is a way of thinking and living. And it is governed by principles clearly stated in the Word of God. The Bible tells us that all the godly leaders of Israel were prosperous and successful (Uzziah, 2 Chronicles 26:5; Jothan, 2 Chronicles 27:6; Hezekiah, 2 Chronicles 31:21 and 32:27-30).

Prosperity is a reward for following God's ways. Psalms 1;23;65;71;112, and Proverbs 3:9,10,16; 4:18; 8:18; 10:22; 11:25,28; 13:22,25; 24:11; 15:6; 19: 17; 21:21; 22:9; 28:20,25,27, all promise the godly prosperity. The prophets—Isaiah 60,65, Jeremiah 33:6-11, Ezekiel 34:25-21; 36:29-30—all say the same thing. In the New Testament, there were many wealthy believers—Nicodemus, Joseph of Arimathea, Cornelius, Candace's treasurer, Mary Magdalene, Joanna (Chuza's wife), Suzanna, Mary of Bethany, etc. Our Lord Jesus Christ himself never lacked. He received great gifts from the magi. He had a home (Mark 2:1); he had a treasury and treasurer, Judas; he travelled in a convoy (Mark 4:36); his robe was fought over by well-paid Roman soldiers; he had many financiers (Luke 8:2-3); and he was buried in a rich man's tomb. This relative material poverty (considering that he is the King of Kings), is for the purpose of making us rich (2 Corinthians 8:9).

At no time was he spiritually poor. In heaven or on earth, he was spiritually rich. He couldn't redeem us if he was spiritually poor—he too would need a redeemer (Matthew 5:3). He voluntarily blame relatively materially poor so that we would become rich—spiritually and materially.

Prosperity

Prosperity is part of the finished work of Jesus Christ. In 3 John 2, we are told that prosperity is God's will for our life. These are the seven laws of prosperity according to the Word of God;

a. work hard (Proverbs 10:4; 12:11)
b. give (Proverbs 3:9-10; 19:17)
c. save (Proverbs 21:20)
d. invest wisely (Proverbs 28:19-20; 21:5)
e. borrow carefully (Proverbs 22:7)
f. avoid unjust gain (Proverbs 17:23; 28:8,16,24)
g. trust the Lord (Proverbs 28:25; 10:22)

There is no way you will not prosper when you follow the Word of God. God challenges you to test him in this matter (Malachi 3:10). We must not allow the enemy to steal our prosperity.

Pray:

In the mighty name of Jesus, I rebuke the devourer. I declare that prosperity is mine as a child of God. I shall prosper in Jesus' name. Amen.

The real reason that the prosperity message has not been universally popular is fear—fear of covetousness, idolatry, love of money, worldliness, and loss of wealth; fear of being unworthy and of what people will say. But what part has fear got to play in the Christian FAITH? Isn't fear the driving force behind ungodliness and the guiding principle of worldliness? The Bible doesn't tell us to run away from anything in fear, certainly not from prosperity. According to the Scriptures, it is fools who do not need prosperity: 'Of what use is money in the hand of a fool?' (Proverbs 17:16, NIV). I can think of a thousand uses for money in the hands of the wise, in the hands of those who are called, for Christ is to us the power of God and wisdom of God (1 Corinthians 1:24). A fool does not need prosperity. He doesn't know God (Psalm 14:1), so money is dangerous in his hands. But prosperity is the birthright of the believer.

Pray:

I am not a fool. I am an elect. Therefore, I will prosper in Jesus' name. Amen.

God is honoured when his people are blessed, prosperous, healthy and happy (2 Corinthians 9:11-12). If you haven't got enough for a certain project, what you have must be a seed. Begin to tithe, begin to give. Begin to put the principle of the seed in operation in your life. That principle is clearly stated in Genesis 1:29, Mark 4:26-32 and 2 Corinthians 9:6-11. God supplies seed to the sower and bread for food. You eat your bread and you sow your seed. If you eat your seed, you have nothing to sow for God to multiply. But if you sow your seed, God promises to multiply and increase the harvest and enrich you liberally for his glory (2 Corinthians 9:10-11). However, the usual complaint is, 'I have done all this, I have given and I haven't received anything back.' Well, the Scriptures cannot be broken. Heaven and earth will pass away, the Word of God will never pass away (Matthew 5:18; 24:35, Mark 13:31, Luke 21:33).

God is not a man that he should lie, or a son of man that he should change his mind. When he speaks, he does it (Numbers 23:19). He delights in fulfiling his Word (Jeremiah 1:12). His Word shall not return to him void. His Word is fully tested and found flawless (Psalm 12:6; 119:140, Proverbs 30:5). So to say that the Word doesn't work is to say in effect that God is a liar. He says, 'Test me' (Malachi 3:10). The real issue is ignorance of the way God works. We expect God to work like the lottery. But he doesn't work that way, though he can if he chooses to. There is no hurry with God. Hurry is the devil. God answers the highest and greatest desires of our heart in his own time and in his own way. Abraham, Isaac, Jacob, Joseph, Moses, David, Paul, etc. had to wait to get some of their prayers answered. Delay is not the same as denial.

God wants us to cleanse ourselves of negativity—fear, doubt, feeling of unworthiness, etc. He wants us to grow spiritually into answered prayers. He wants us to grow to the point of receiving the answer. The patriarchs had to do this. Abraham had to learn not to fear. Isaac had to learn not to run from challenges. Jacob had to learn not to deceive. Joseph had to learn not to be arrogant. Moses had to learn not to be impatient. David had to learn not to lust. Paul had to learn not to rely on his achievements. What do you need to learn? Ask yourself that today. Learn what you need to learn, and gradually, naturally, simply, yet surely, the answers will come (Mark 4:27-28). God makes everything beautiful in its own time (Ecclesiastes 3:11).

Pray like this:

Lord, I am the clay and you are the potter. Make me into the kind of person you want me to be. In Jesus' name. Amen.

No one has to be poor unless they have resigned themselves to that imagined fate. God is a faith God. Never live by what you see but by what God says. The fact that God says something doesn't mean your faith will not be challenged or tested. That is when to show your faith. Faith is very patient (Hebrews 6:12). Fear and unbelief, of course, are always in a hurry. You are who God says you are, regardless of your present circumstances. You are strong, not weak. You are fruitful, not barren. You are the head, not the tail. You are above, not beneath. Faith is agreeing with God. Fear is agreeing with the enemy. Present circumstances cannot stop you from becoming who God says you are. My brothers and sisters, the Bible is a genuine record of people's experience with God (see Job 5:27, Psalm 37:25-26). God is not a trickster. That is the devil's job. That is what it means to be a devil—a devil is a worker of lies. God is a God of truth. In him is no crookedness or perversity. He is holy, just and righteous. His eyes are too pure to behold iniquity (Habakkuk 1:13). Nothing can stop the fulfilment of God's plan for your life as long as you trust him.

You won't become who God wants to make you overnight. And if you do, it will be a very long night, as someone has said. When you start to follow God wholeheartedly, he will get you to your destiny. The enemy is simply a liar. He will keep repeating his lies hoping you will believe them. Pay him no attention. If God is for you, nothing can be against you. No devil is strong enough to frustrate God's will. Anyone who tries to do so, will be shattered into a thousand pieces (Isaiah 8:9-10). When it comes to power, forget about Satan. Deception is evidence of powerlessness. God is the superintendent of his plans for your life, not you. The buck stops with him. It is not your job to make it happen (Isaiah 46:10, Jeremiah 1:12). With him is no variation or shifting shadow. Never look at anything as a block to your destiny. That is apostasy. Nothing can block the fulfilment of your destiny. Not by might, not by human power, but by the Spirit of God. Every mountain shall be removed as surely as heaven rules (Zechariah 4:6-7). Do not give too close a study to present circumstances by dwelling on apparent limitations. Focus on the Word of God instead.

The person who dwells on apparent limitations soon becomes the 'I can't' person. They accept limitations, wrap up their talents, and hide then away in the apparent limitations. Success becomes impossible. Poverty becomes inevitable. And the enemy leads the chorus in hell, 'another one bites the dust.' This is not the will of God. If we persevere, success and victory will come (Hebrews 10:35-37). The soul established in faith accepts the promises of God. It is strong enough to put them to work and patient enough to wait for the result. To man is given the highest power, that is, faith in the Word of God. With it, man is able to exercise dominion over the devil and his cohorts. Whatever we bind on earth shall be bound in heaven; whatever we loose on earth shall be loose in heaven. These are the keys of the kingdom. When man's soul is lifted by faith in the promises of God, nothing becomes impossible (Matthew 21:21-22, Mark 11:22-24). There are two omnipotent things in the universe: Mark 10:27 tells us that all things are possible with God, and Mark 9:23 tells us that all things are possible to the one who believes.

The Scriptures cannot be broken. When faith is resident in the soul, we are positive, confident and restful. Our soul is full of light and there is lightness in our spirit. The enemy is repelled. The just shall live by faith is the key principle of the Christian life (Habakkuk 2:4, Romans 1:17, Galatians 3:11, Hebrews 10:38). By faith, we consciously bring ourselves under the control of the law of life (Romans 8:2) resulting in joy and peace (Romans 8:6). The law of life lifts us up while the law of death pulls us down. The law of death is the law of fear (Hebrews 2:15). It brings darkness, slavery and oppression. It results in failure, sickness and poverty. It is what the enemy uses to steal. We must not permit this in our life. Life, liberty, prosperity, health and the pursuit of happiness are the inalienable rights of man, and they should never be surrendered to anyone, talk less, the enemy. Never give anything up on your right to prosper. Never allow the thief to steal even a hoof from you!

Pray:

God has given me everything pertaining to life and godliness. I refuse to submit to the enemy's lies. I claim my prosperity in Jesus' name. Amen.

The Opposer

1 Peter 5:8 tells us, *'Be of sober spirit, be on the alert'*. Sobriety and alertness are indispensable for a Christian. There are some who have arrived at the strange conclusion that there is no devil and there is no evil. Only good, only God is what there is in the universe. Apart from the clear lack of scriptural support for such assertions, the enemy himself would really love to be left alone to carry on his dastardly activities. The Bible tells us to be sober (self controlled) and alert, for there is an enemy, whom we have been chosen to resist and trample upon (1 Peter 5:8-9; Luke 10:19). We are God's army and he commands us to wage war on ungodliness and its architect. We are God's battle axe, God's shatterer, God's war club, and God's weapon of war (Jeremiah 51:20).

The rebellion of Lucifer happened before the creation of man. Man is God's kick in the teeth of Satan. Man is God's slap in the face of the enemy. Man is God's spit in the eye of the adversary. Lucifer decided to take control of heaven but was expelled. He and his demons came down to earth to set up a rebel territory in this corner of the universe, as an outpost of darkness and evil to challenge God. But God had better ideas. He made Adam and Eve, you and me. 'Rule', he says. 'Have dominion'. Satan and his hordes may be lurking around the planet, but dominion belongs to man. *'rule thou in the midst of thine enemies'* (Psalm 110:2, KJV). Man has been chosen before the foundation of the world in Christ (2 Timothy 1:9), to teach Satan a lesson (Ephesians 3:10)—that rebellion is folly. God is too powerful to fight Satan.

We have been chosen to teach the rebels the lesson that God wants to teach them. It is not about power. It is about wisdom. Satan needs to be shown to the whole universe to be a fool, and God's righteousness, wisdom and justice vindicated. Though the deceiver deceived Eve, and Adam (though not deceived, 1 Timothy 2:14) chose to go with his wife, Satan is still in trouble (Revelations 20:10). He will be destroyed. He corrupted his wisdom and became a fool (Ezekiel 28:17). He has been committing acts of folly ever since (1 Corinthians 2:8). Iniquity, rebellion and evil are acts of folly. He was created perfect in wisdom and beauty. But he allowed himself to become the originating fountain of evil, iniquity, violence and unrighteousness (Ezekiel 28:15). He become the first sinner, liar and murderer (John 8:44, 1 John 3:8). What folly.

Though he is still deceiving many today to follow his lies, the fact remains that Jesus has conquered. Christ has overcome, and Satan's days are numbered and very short. He cannot and will not escape his destiny, for Topheth has been made ready for the king of evil (Isaiah 30:33); God has made it deep and large for Satan and his demons. They will burn. They should burn. Our job is to put Satan in his place. That is the purpose of this book—to expose and shame the enemy, bless man and glorify God. Man is Satan's nemesis. It is Christ, as man that broke Satan back (John 12:31), and it is the body of Christ that has the job of rubbing Satan's face in the mud (Malachi 4:3, Micah 7:10, Zechariah 20:5, Luke 10:19). We are Satan's worst nightmare. Pride can endure anything except humiliation, shame and disgrace. That is exactly what we have been elected to do to Satan—disgrace him. Christ has already overpowered, plundered and disarmed him (Luke 11:22). Our job is to rub salt into his wounds. And pride cannot take that. So he fights back, like a wounded beast. Moreover, we are going to enjoy heaven and inherit the earth, while he is going to burn. So he hates us the more. That however is his problem. We don't like him too. In fact, we don't care a hoot about him, expect to inflict what God has commanded us to inflict on him. Nothing we do to him in time can adequately pay him for all the evil he has caused. But eternity will take care of him.

The Enemy's Tactics

We've seen why he hates us. Let's look at how he fights and opposes us. The people of God had to take on the enemy before they could possess the Promised Land. David had many battles with the enemy to establish Israel as a strong nation, with Jerusalem as its capital. Perhaps the best panorama of the enemy's warfare tactics against the saints, as we do God's work, is provided in the book of Nehemiah. In that book, we see the faces of the adversary.

We see him resisting God and the truth. We see him in his selfishness, subjecting people to his evil. We see him mocking God's people as a means of gaining an advantage. We see him hating, despising and reproaching God's people. We see him raging, slandering, annoying, conspiring, hindering, scheming, lying, tempting, infiltrating and corrupting God's people. We see him using fear, intimidation and aggression against God's people. We also see him plotting violence to disturb and stop God's work. He failed of course. Hallelujah!

This is the creature we have been called to deal with. Never forget though, that Christ has won the victory. It isn't our job to win the victory. Ours is the easy part. Easy does it. Our part is to enforce the victory. We are unassailable, impregnable and invincible (Isaiah 33:16). The Church is heavily defended. Those with us are more than those who are with the enemy (2 Kings 6:16), and it is impossible for us to be taken by assault (Matthew 16:18, John 1:5). If God were to open your spiritual eyes and reveal to you, as he has done to me in his mercy oftentimes, the nature of our defense, you will begin to treat Satan and his demons as the things of mockery that they really are (Job 5:22, Jeremiah 10:15). They are of no account, utterly worthless, and destined to perish (Isaiah 41:24,29; 51:7,8,12,13). *'Where is the fury of the oppressor?'* (Isaiah 51:13). When he has finished roaring and barking, what can he do? Let him do something instead of just barking, so that we may fear him (Isaiah 41:23).

He is a nonentity, a complete fraud. This book is not to glorify him. We are here to say what the Word of God says about him. As someone has said, it isn't a question of whether you will have to deal with Satan. You will have to deal with him. The issue is knowing how to deal with him, and this is the purpose of this book. You will have to learn how the people of God have dealt with him, shamed him and fed him with dung and mud (Psalm 83: 9-10, Malachi 2:3).

So in Nehemiah, we see the enemy opposing God's work. In chapter 4, verse 11, the enemy states his purpose clearly: to infiltrate, to kill and to stop God's work. But the dreamer didn't succeed in doing any of these. Jesus says the enemy comes to kill, to steal and to destroy (John 10:10). Here, in Nehemiah, we have it straight from the horse's mouth (or is it the serpent's mouth?). The enemy said the same thing in Exodus 15:9, KJV: *'I will pursue, I will overtake, I will divide the spoil; my lust shall be satisfied upon them; I will draw my sword, my hand shall destroy them'*. But verse 10 tells us God's answer: *'Thou didst blow with thy wind, the sea covered them: they sank as lead in the mighty waters'*. *'Who is like unto thee, O LORD, among the gods?'* says verse 11,12, *'who is like thee, glorious in holiness, fearful in praises, doing wonders? Thou stretchedst out thy right hand, the earth swallowed them'*. You will have to learn to deal with the enemy as a child of God (verse 13). The battle belongs to the Lord. You will have to deal wit the enemy as a redeemed, saved, justified, sanctified, Spirit-filled, accepted, beloved, safe and secure child of God. With this attitude, the enemy cannot win. Trusting and relying fully on the love and power of God (Exodus 15:13), the enemy has only to fear, tremble, be in dread, terror and anguish and be dismayed (verse 14-16).

Satan is a selfish being. He loves no one and cares for no one. His five 'I will' statements in Isaiah 14:13-14 reveal his heart of selfishness. This is what we see in Nehemiah 2:10. The enemy was very displeased that Nehemiah had come to seek the well-being if God's people who, we are told in 1:3, were in great distress and adversity. The enemy doesn't care if anyone is in adversity. The lunatic actively seeks to cause people adversity. He is the enemy of good. He is the wicked one. He is evil through and through. Selfishness is a chief characteristic of Satan and his agents. We can see what selfishness has done to our world. It is the chief principle of Satanism. It doesn't exist in God's thoughts. Selfishness, self-reliance, self-centredness, self-aggrandizement and self-seeking are of the enemy. The first demonstration of it is in Genesis 47. Before that, Genesis 1 shows us that there is no reason for selfishness on earth. God made everything in abundance (Psalm 104: 1-23), he takes care of his creation and he is utterly dependable. All the patriarchs enjoyed his blessings, his power of well-being. There was assurance that God will take care of his creation.

But the devil, through his type, the pharaoh, introduced selfishness into the world's consciousness and the world has never been the same again. Genesis is the book of beginnings, and chapter 41 tells us about how the organisation and governing of society by selfishness began. We see Pharaoh, the devil's man, having a dream, getting scared and hiring Joseph to manage, control and monopolize the world's resources for him. The lie of scarcity—the principle, notion, belief and myth of 'everyone for himself' and 'every nation for itself'—had begun. The world economy, as well as biblical faith, was saddled with the lie that God can't take good care of his creation. "If you don't join the rat race, and grab as much as you can, you will end up with nothing", the devil says. The only thing about the rat race is that everyone in the race is a rat. But we have been called to a higher life. Our God is a God of abundance. He will prosper his people. Self-seeking, toiling and grabbing can add nothing to his blessings. God wants us to work hard, use our talents and be productive, but he doesn't want us to toil, rely on our-selves and be self-centred (Psalm 127:2). Proverbs 10:22 states clearly, *'It is the blessing of the Lord that makes one rich'*. Toiling adds nothing to it. The enemy whispers into your ears, "Everyone is grabbing. If you don't grab now, who will take care of you when you are old?"

Tell him to worry about his own future, not yours. Selfishness as a creed was introduced into the world by the devil. The monopolist pharaoh took the people's money (Genesis 47:13-26), then their livestock, then their land. Before long, they were selling themselves to him as slaves—economic slavery. However, real power isn't in the hands of those who grab and monopolise resources. Real power is in the hands of those who trust God's abun-dance, blessing and power of well-being (Exodus 12:31-36, Genesis 47:27). Our well-being cannot be taken from us— ever (Romans 8:3, 5, 7, Psalm 119:112). God is the guar-antor of his children's well-being. There is no need to fear, worry or pay attention to Satan's lies. Selfishness isn't an option for God's people. We are here to rearrange the world, as Jesus did when he was here. We are the light of the world and the salt of the earth. We are not here to be conditioned by the world, but to change it (Jeremiah 15:19). We must not turn to the world. They must turn to us. Satan is profane, according to Ezekiel 28:16. To be profane means to be flat, empty, exhausted and one-dimensional. He has nothing to offer. We have a lot to offer the world, starting with love. Selfishness is of the enemy and has no part in the Christian life.

Pray:

O Lord, rid me of all selfish tendencies, in the name of Jesus. Amen.

So in Nehemiah 2:10, we see the selfish one in operation. He doesn't want anyone to be happy, because happiness isn't possible for him. He can't be happy, so he doesn't want anyone to be happy. Well, he cannot control our choices. Our happiness doesn't depend on him. We choose to be happy, and there is nothing he can do about it (Psalm 89:15). Because of the enemy's selfishness, he seeks to put people in bondage. We must frustrate him. It displeased him greatly that a deliverer had come to help God's people and set them free. So he began his nefarious activities to subvert the good purposes of God. In Daniel 10:13, we see him opposing Daniel's effort on behalf of the suffering nation of Israel. In Acts 13, we see another agent of the enemy in the person of Elymas, coming forward to oppose Paul and Barnabas as they preach the gospel in Paphos. The proconsul wanted to hear the Word of God, verse 7, but the enemy showed up his ugly face. In verse 8, we see the enemy actively opposing the gospel and seeking to turn the proconsul away from the truth. But Paul fixed his gaze upon him and filled with the Holy Spirit, he gave us another portrait of the enemy verse 9-10—worker of all deceit and fraud; slanderer; accuser; liar; enemy of all righteousness; perverter of the right ways of the Lord.

The Holy Spirit summarily dealt with the no-good thing (verse 11). Then the proconsul believed. We still have to deal with the enemy this way time and again, as we advance the kingdom of God on earth. He will always show up anywhere the good news is being preached and the good work of God is being done. And summary judgement must be meted out to the foul spirit. In 1 Thessalonians 2:18, Paul again tells us of the hindering work of the enemy. He had planned to visit the Thessalonians, but Satan opposed him. This is what Satan does. He is the opposer. He has set himself up as the adversary of God and man—of good, righteousness and truth (5:7). We must trample upon him without mercy. Anyone who seeks to spread evil on this earth and oppose good must be dealt with as they deserve. We are not in the business of tolerating evil, talk less, compromising with it. In Nehemiah, we see the enemy opposing Nehemiah and seeking to disgrace him with God's people (Nehemiah 1:3; 2:17; 6:13). Satan plans nothing but disgrace for the servants of God. He cannot bear to see us honoured.

In Acts 28, we see Satan planning to bring about a disgraceful end to Paul's life. Paul had survived a shipwreck on his way to Rome, and landed of the Mediterranean island of Malta. But Satan was already making his plans. Verse 3 tells us that Satan had hidden a viper nearby. As Paul gathered a bundle of sticks and laid them on the fire, the viper came out and bit Paul. Satan's plan was to bring about a shameful end to this great apostle's life. Abraham, Isaac, Jacob, Moses, Joshua, Samuel, David, the prophets, the Baptist, etc., all died honourably. Jesus died and rose again in triumph. How is it that the greatest apostle of Christendom should die in disgrace, bitten by a snake despite the promises of God to his servants concerning victory over the serpent, Satan? Should a serpent now end Paul's life? Should Satan be handed a propaganda victory? No. Never. The enemy is the one that will perish disgracefully, not God's servants. But the natives had already come to their conclusion. The slanderer was at work. Paul had to be a murderer (verse 4).

That is all the enemy seeks—to find you guilty. That is the reason he slanders and accuses. The sinner from the beginning seeks to paint everybody as guilty. But the Bible says, *'Who will bring a charge against God's elect?'* (Romans 8:33). God is the one who justifies. The liar was quickly shown to be what he is. Verse 5 tells us that Paul shook the creature off his hands into the fire and he suffered no harm. It is the same fire that provides you comfort that will destroy your enemy in Jesus' name. Instead of disgrace, Paul was vindicated. He is a man of God (verse 6). All those who have uttered the enemy's lies against us will sing a new tune in Jesus' name. The agents of the enemy will perish with him unless they repent. Woe is their portion. God has cursed them and we pronounce them cursed, in the name of the Lord. May the curse of the Lord be upon all their wicked works. May they not prosper, in Jesus' name. Amen.

A servant of God cannot be disgraced. It is impossible. The work of God was advanced on Malta. There were healings, deliverances and conversions on the island (verse 7-9). The name of the Lord was glorified. The man of God was honoured and blessed materially. The enemy was trounced. This is the truth of the gospel of God. *'Let God arise, let His enemies be scattered, And let those who hate Him flee before Him... But let the righteous be glad; let them exult before God; Yes, let them rejoice with gladness'* (Psalm 68:1-3). Satan's end is disgrace. God has promised that (Isaiah 14:16). Our end is peace and glory. Amen. The enemy also tried but failed to disgrace Nehemiah. His tactics haven't changed, and the result will continue to be the same: Satan will constantly be humiliated and God, along with his people, will be honoured forever. Let us trust God to disgrace our enemy.

The enemy also sought to use mockery as a weapon (Nehemiah 2:19; 4:1-3). He uses his demons to mock our salvation, redemption and position in Christ. Let them mock as long as they want. Just make sure you hear as if you don't hear. Treat them as if they are not even speaking. As long as their hatred and anger doesn't affect you, you are a winner. When they insult you, rejoice (Matthew 5:11-12). You are blessed, and they can't stand it. When the enemy annoys and seeks to provoke you, laugh it off. Laughter is one of the greatest weapons against the adversary. He has no answer to it and often flees. If you feel demoralized, seek the strength of the Lord immediately (Nehemiah 4:5 and 1 Chronicles 16:11).

When the enemy sees that you are marching on, he gets dirty (Nehemiah 4:8), but don't be concerned. Pray and march on by all means necessary (Nehemiah 4:9). Remember, if you stop, he wins. So don't give up. The enemy's aggression must be met by fire for fire. Prayer is our intercontinental ballistic missile. It gets anyone, anywhere. Pray with your shield of faith held high (Ephesians

6:16-18). Never cave in to fear (Nehemiah 4:14). In war, fear is a prominent factor for both sides of the opposing nations. To be a hero means to be fearless—not afraid of failing because failure is not an option. Satan will try to scare you, I promise you. He will (see Nehemiah 6:9, 13, 14, 19). If you let him scare you, these are the results:

a. He will replace God in your life with himself and separate you from God.

b. He will ruin your testimony.

c. He will steal your peace and joy.

d. He will cause confusion, frustration, distraction, anger, hostility and wrong relationships in your life.

e. He will steal the blessings promised to you by God.

f. He will thwart God's purposes and plans for your life.

g. He will mess up and destroy so much of your life.

h. He will destroy everything good in your life.

i. He will bring fatigue, worry, busyness, noise, hurry and crowd into your life to wear you down and out.

j. He will cheat God of any glory in your life, and…

k. he will ultimately destroy you.

So you can see that fear is not an option Nehemiah 6:11. With the wicked and uncompromising evil designs of the enemy, war is the only option for anyone who wants anything good in this life. There can be no compromise with the enemy. All you need to do is to remember God's justice (Nehemiah 4:4-5); remember God's protection (Nehemiah 4:9); remember God's power (Nehemiah 4:14);

and remember God's commitment (Nehemiah 4:20)—and fight! We see the enemy using all sorts of tactics to try to stop Nehemiah. Persistence is Satan's main approach. He never gives up trying to get us to give up. If one thing doesn't work, he tries another. But no matter how the enemy approaches, we must be determined to beat him. He will try to get you to fight him on the basis of his lies, but we must fight him with our own weapons and rules of engagement. Never fight the enemy according to his own rules. They are all rigged in his favour. Satan is a liar. You must fight him with God's truth.

No matter the difficulty, the work must go on. Aluta Continua, Victoria Aceta—the battle continues, but victory is certain. Crows only pick at the best fruit, which is why the enemy is attacking you. You have a great future in the Lord, so onward Christian soldier. The enemy devised all sorts of schemes against Nehemiah, but to no avail (Nehemiah 6:1-2). The answer remains the same: '*Why should the work stop...?*' (verse 3). Why should the work of righteousness stop? It is the enemy that needs to stop his evil. The people of God are not going to be distracted from the great work of advancing the kingdom of God.

Then the enemy tried slander and accusations of demagogy (Nehemiah 2:19; 6:6-7). The enemy knows that believers are righteous people, yet he accuses and slanders persistently. Don't let this trouble you. Our cause is just and our conscience is clear. Jesus says in John 8:44 that the enemy is a liar. That settles it, doesn't it? The accusations of the enemy are part of his psychological warfare against believers. They are calculated to scare, discourage, weaken and paralyse (Nehemiah 6:9). Satan is the accuser of the brethren (Revelations 12:10). We need a thick skin to ensure that his lies don't bother us, for that is what they are—just lies (Nehemiah 6:8). Keep a clear conscience before the Lord always (verse 9). He will fulfil his purpose (Nehemiah 6:16). Do not allow the enemy to tempt you to compromise in any way (Nehemiah 6:13).

So despite all his different approaches, the opposer was beaten, and the wall was completed (Nehemiah 6:15). Verse 16 tells us that the enemy lost his confidence because of what God had done for his people in a record time of fifty-two days. When we don't lose our confidence, the enemy loses his—period. So be strong in the Lord, and in the power of his might. The opposer was routed. A mighty fortress is our God, indeed. God's purpose is not to bypass difficulty but to transform difficulty so that we will say that this work was done with the Lord's help (Nehemiah 6:16). The enemy was routed and badly shaken. He tried other tactics but Nehemiah had tasted blood (Numbers 23:24, Deuteronomy 33:26-29), and was not going to be beaten. The enemy tried infiltration, pollution and corruption (Nehemiah 13:4-5); neglect of God's house (Nehemiah 13:10-13); disregarding the Sabbath (Nehemiah 13:15-22); unequal yoke (Nehemiah 13:23-27). But in all these things Nehemiah proved more than a conqueror! With Christ's armour, the opposer is certain to be disgraced in your life too.

Pray:

In the mighty name of Jesus, I declare that I am more than a conqueror. No weapons fashioned by the enemy against me shall prosper. Amen.

The Tempter

*T*he enemy is not just seeking to induce thoughts. He is looking for action. Bad thoughts should not be entertained anyway, but what the enemy is really looking for is action. The reason he brings evil thoughts to people's minds and says evil things is for the purpose of eliciting an evil act on the part of the person. As long as his thoughts are not acted upon, they are nothing; they come from nothing and will return into nothingness. Only the thoughts of God will stand. God's thoughts are contained in his Word, and they are the only thing that will endure (Matthew 24:35). This is not to say that evil thoughts should be entertained. This is not right inner culture. God tells us what he wants us to think about (Philippians 4:8). The enemy, however, is really looking for action.

Every evil thought or picture that he brings into our mind and every lie he whispers are followed by evil suggestions. He operates by evil logic. He always follows up his lies with evil counsel. That is what he is really looking for. He wants you to do so and so, for such and such reason. He cannot make anyone do anything, so he acts by persuasion (Galatians 5:7-9). A little leaven, leavens the whole lump of dough, says verse 9. The enemy works by trying to persuade you of his lies, so that you will do what he suggests. This is the face of Satan as tempter. He has absolutely no God-given power over anyone. Roman 6:16 says that when you present yourselves to someone as slaves of obedience, you are slaves of the one whom you obey. The enemy wants you to be so convinced of his lies that you present yourself to him as a slave for obedience. And what a cruel taskmaster the foul thing of darkness is. It is not our job to obey him.

We are the legitimate governors of earth. He is a thief—a shattered and broken thief (John 12:31). He is not entitled to anyone's attention, talk less, obedience. He and his hordes are rebels against truth and should be treated with contempt. Do not let him persuade you or anything. Do not let him tell you anything, and do not let him force you to choose how you think about anything. Your thoughts are your private affair, your innermost possession, and the enemy must be kept away from them. He belongs under your feet, not under your scalp. If you have anything to say to him, write it under the sole of an old pair of shoes. He will get it alright. Cast down his own thoughts, get on with your life and don't reason with him—ever.

Eve

Eve was someone who allowed the tempter into her thoughts. The enemy approached her (Genesis 3), and as usual, he posed a question. When the enemy wants to rob believers of spiritual vitality, joy and peace, he poses a question. The purpose of the question is to create doubt and set in motion a process of inward questioning, disputing, rationalizing and calculating. The tempter seeks to engage you in a dialogue of questions, a discussion of lies, and a deliberation of futile imaginations. He seeks to get you involved in inward thinking and reasoning with him. God expressly forbids this. In Philippians 2:14, we are commanded to do all things without disputing, doubting and inner questioning. 2 Corinthians 10:5 tells us to cast down every argument, calculation and computation, and take them captive to the word of Christ. We have no business trying to provide an answer to the liar's questions. Let him answer them himself. The Bible tells us not to pay attention to Satan and his demons—his horde of deceitful and seducing spirit (1 Timothy 4:1). We are not interested in their arguments and perverted logic. Everything they say or suggest is perverse, crooked, wrong and the opposite of truth. In Acts 20:29-30, Paul warns us of these savage wolves. They speak perverse things to draw away believers and lead them astray. Don't let anyone lead you astray with empty philosophy and high sounding evil nonsense, Paul says in Colossians 2:8.

So Satan approached Eve with his nonsensical question, and she decided the serpent was worth a hearing. The Bible tells us in Ezekiel 28:17 that Satan is a fool operating on corrupted wisdom. Now the Bible also tells us how to answer a fool's question. Proverbs 26:5 tells us to answer a fool as his folly deserves, lest he be wise in his own eyes. Do not answer him according to his folly, lest you also be like him, says verse 4. Eve decided to answer the fool according to his folly and she became a fallen creature like him. She should have ignored him, as his folly deserves. Talking to Satan only encourages him. He likes Christians to talk to him, and he really loves Christians to reason with him. I say ignore the foul thing. There may be few occasions that you speak the Word of God to the liar to rebuke him. But as a rule, ignore him, as 1 Timothy 4:1 commands.

From the moment Eve began to dialogue with the liar, he received the encouragement he needed to proceed with his evil work. To ignore him is to cut him short and send him running. Remember, Satan's questions are intended to create doubt. In Eve's case, it was meant to cause distrust in God's character, and Eve swallowed the bait. The direct challenge to God's Word followed in Genesis 3:4. When the enemy lies, he is careful to locate his lies in the future where the results cannot be checked presently. He wants you to act now on his lies about the future or about something you cannot immediately perceive. There was no way for Eve to know whether or not she would die until she ate the fruit, and that is how the liar works. Eve died, and billions have died as a result of Satan's lies. The results are in the past, and we can check it. Never listen to Satan or his demons.

From the moment Eve believed Satan's lies, she had no defense against lust. Lust is not the reason she fell. Lust is common, according to Jesus in Matthew 5:28. The defense against lust or any other sin is to believe that what God says is true. Eve chose to believe the enemy's lies instead, and she acted out her lust—of the flesh, the eyes and the pride of life (verse 6). The result was tragic. There is no need to elaborate on this—every evil thing that the world has known is the result of that act. The tempter is tempting people today. He is still at work, tempting Christians and non-Christians, to act out of his own intentions. Your job is to make sure that you don't. The tempter tried to do the same thing to our Lord Jesus Christ. But Jesus was no Eve.

In Matthew 4, after the Lord had been baptised and filled with the Holy Spirit, he departed into the wilderness. He fasted for forty days and forty nights, and he became hungry (verse 2). 'If you are the Son of God, command that these stones become bread,' said the liar. Notice the question again. That is always his approached. Jesus knew he was the Son of God. He knew it from the Spirit (Matthew 3:17); he knew it from the Scriptures (Psalm 40:7, Hebrews 10:7); he knew it from eternity. No amount of satanic 'ifs' would cause him to doubt that fact. Satan was no match for this champion. The liar tried the lust of the flesh, as with Eve, and failed. He tried the lust of the eyes, with the same result. Then he tried the boastful pride of life, but was beaten again. This victor knew his Father and wasn't going to worship any liar. The tempter fled in disgrace (Matthew 4:11), no match for the redeemer of mankind.

Pray:

Let every evil arrow of temptation receive the fire of God, in the mighty name of Jesus. Amen.

As an essentially broken entity, all the enemy has left are lies. So he tempts people to do his bidding by deceiving them. He cannot, however, make anyone do anything. We are free-thinking and free-acting beings with the full powers of choice, made in the image of God. Our freewill is the instrument of dominion, by which we govern ourselves and our world. Satan wasn't given any such authority, so he needs deception. Christ tells us to pray against yielding to temptations. The average Christian is not tempted to kill, but we are all tempted to lie, cheat, lust, etc. Let us not yield to any of these. A little leaven leavens the whole lump of dough (1 Corinthians 5:6). We usually talk about falling into sin, but no one falls into sin. That is impossible. People usually creep into sin. Everyone is tempted when he is enticed by his own lust (James 1:14). Sin only results after the gradual and full conception of lust (verse 15).

The enemy has so many tools with which to entice and tempt believers. The media is chief among these. Television, newspapers and magazines are full of lewd images. No part of the body is considered 'private' any-more. Consumerism and debt provide temptation to steal. Homosexuality is now being preached from the pulpit! Paul says in 1 Thessalonians 3:5 that the tempter is after our faith. Keep watching and praying, Jesus says, that you may not yield to temptation (Matthew 26:41). Self-control is needed in this regard (1 Corinthians 7:5). But we have God's assurance that he will not allow us to enter into over-whelming temptation, but will provide escape and deliver-ance for his people (1 Corinthians 10:13, 2 Peter 2:9). To be tempted itself is not sin. It is yielding to the temptation that is sin. That is part of what resisting the enemy means. We should not tempt God either, as the enemy sought to do in Matthew 4. Prayer is the best defense against temptation. In Luke 22:31-32, Jesus said that Satan has asked for per-mission to tempt Peter, but he had prayed for Peter. The enemy was after Peter's faith (1 Thessalonians 3:5), but Jesus had prayed for Peter. It was no longer a question of 'if' but 'when'. Peter was of course tempted (Matthew 26: 69-75), and he fell away, contrary to his declarations in Matthew 26:33—his problem was self-confidence. But Christ had prayed and Peter was restored in John 21:15-17.

The temptation of David, serves best to illustrate the gradual conception of lust. David had accumulated wives, contrary to God's command in Deuteronomy 17:17. 2 Samuel 3:2-5 lists six of David's wives. Some were undoubtedly political marriages, but David was contravening the Word of God. He was entertaining lust. He acquired more wives and concubines in Jerusalem (2 Samuel 5:13), and in 2 Samuel 11, lust had fully conceived in David. Instead of going to war, he sent Joab and others, and he stayed at Jerusalem (verse 1). Enter Bathsheba—the enemy's bait to break David in his middle prosperous age (verse 2). Bathsheba was beautiful, and David had to have her. Despite being the wife of one of his soldiers (verse 3), he had her brought to him and he lay with her. When he found out she was pregnant, he had her husband murdered, and then he took her for his wife (2 Samuel 11: 5-27). But the results were disastrous. David knew no peace for a year (Psalm 32:3), and his health suffered (Psalm 32:4). But that was just the beginning. In 2 Samuel 12, God sent Prophet Nathan to challenge David, and there began David's decline. The sword would not depart from David's house (verse 10), and David suffered terribly. The child died (verse 18), and more disasters followed. Amnon, David's first-born, raped his half sister, Tamar (2 Samuel 13:32). Absalom become estranged from David, returned to Jerusalem, and led a coup d'état that nearly cost David his life (2 Samuel 13:37-20:3). Absalom raped his father's wives during the uprising, was left hanging, and then murdered (2 Samuel 16:9-15), causing David more grief. Later, Solomon, Bathsheba's son, had Adonijah killed (1 Kings 2:24-25). Solomon then followed his father's polygamy, married foreign women and practised idolatry, for which he incurred God's wrath (1 Kings 11:1-13). After Solomon's death the kingdom was divided, and more troubles followed.

It is mind-boggling that so much evil could attend the yielding to temptation. No wonder Christ commands us to pray daily against yielding to temptation. The enemy tempts us daily so that we do his bidding and incur God's wrath. Let us learn from David and watch and pray against temptation. Let us lay aside every encumbrance, and the sin which so easily entangles us, and let us run with endurance the race that is set before us, fixing our eyes on Jesus, the author and finisher of our faith (Hebrews 12:1-2).

Pray:

O Lord, strengthen me against the tempter, in Jesus' name. Amen.

Our Lord was tempted in every way, not just in the garden. Yet he was sinless (Hebrews 4:15). He promises to aid us in our battle against the tempter (verse 16). Joseph was a man that knew how to handle temptation. He was seduced by Potiphar's wife, but fearing God, he fled (Genesis 39:7-12). Achan yielded to covetousness, and brought ruin to himself and his household (Joshua 7).

Judas yielded to selfish ambition and destroyed himself. Ananias and Saphira yielded to dishonesty and lost their lives. Samson yielded to lust and careless arrogance (Judges 16:20, and his career was cut short. Saul yielded to rebellion and insubordination, and he lost the kingdom (1 Samuel 15:23). Jacob brought much heartache to himself due to unbrokenness. Lot yielded to worldliness and lost his wife, children and possessions. Absalom's problem was lust for power. Elijah yielded to fear and self-pit, and abandoned his ministry for a while. Abraham yielded to family pressures time and again. Moses yielded to anger, and was promptly called home. Jonah yielded to resentment and hatred and nearly lost his life. James and John yielded to ambition. Timothy yielded to timidity time and time again (2 Timothy 1:7). Rehoboam yielded to immaturity and his kingdom was divided. Uzziah yielded to pride and got leprosy. Asa yielded to self-reliance and died of his disease. Hezekiah yielded to exhibitionism and lost his treasures. Manasseh yielded to the devil and ruined the nation! The Bible is very candid about the faults of its heroes. All these things happened to them as an example, and they were written for our instruction (1 Corinthians 10:11) that we should not crave evil things as they also craved (verse 6). Let us not crave the devil's meat, in Jesus' name.

Pray:

Father God, strengthen me against the flesh, the world and the devil, In Jesus' name. Amen.

The flesh speaks hesitation, double-mindedness, wrong desires, laziness, etc. The world speaks pride, covetousness, self-reliance, self-glorification, etc. The devil speaks confusion, uncertainty, ungodliness, doubt, fear, discouragement, discomfort, iniquity, etc. But the Spirit speaks clarity, certainty, peace, joy, comfort, hope, love, assurance, victory, righteousness, confidence, security and well-being. Let us present ourselves to righteousness, joy, peace, sanctification and eternal life (Romans 6:19-22; 13:12-14; 14:17).

Pray:

I yield myself to the Holy Spirit as a servant of righteousness. I reject every work of darkness, in Jesus' name. Amen.

The Accuser

SIX

The Bible tells us that Satan is the accuser. Revelation 12:10-11 tells us he accuses the brethren before God day and night but was overcome by the word of their testimony about what the blood has done for them. What the Bible says the blood of Jesus has done for us is the perfect answer to Satan's accusations. The accuser wants the believer condemned as guilty, but this is impossible. John 3:18 says he who believes in Jesus is not condemned; he who does not believe has been condemned already because he has not believed in the name of the only begotten Son of God. *'There is therefore now no condemnation to those who are in Christ Jesus'* (Romans 8:1, NKJV). *'Who will bring a charge against God's elect? God is the one who justifies'* (Romans 8:33). Colossians 1:22 says Christ's death freed us from accusations and reproach.

This is at the heart of salvation. Salvation is deliverance from the penalty, the power and ultimately the presence of sin. The Bible says that we have been delivered from the penalty of sin. John 3:16 says, *'For God so loved the world, that He gave His only begotten Son, that whoever believes in Him shall not perish, but have eternal life'*. John 1:12 says,

> *'But to as many as did receive and welcome Him, He gave the authority (power, privilege, right) to become the children of God, that is, to those who believe in (adhere to, trust in, and rely on) His name'* (AMP).

1 John 5:13 says, *'These things I have written to you who believe in the name of the Son of God, so that you may know that you have eternal life'*. The gospel is simple. Jesus came to pay for our sins, which have separated us from God, so that we may be reconciled with God and receive eternal life. Eternal life is the life of God (John 17:3), and comes from knowing God and being reconciled to him.

2 Corinthians 5:19 says that God was in Christ reconciling the world to himself, not counting their trespasses against them. This is salvation. *'He made Him who knew no sin to be sin on our behalf, so that we might become the righteousness of God in Him'* (2 Corinthians 5:21). 1 Corinthians 15:1-4 tells us what the gospel of our salvation is.

> *'Now I make known to you, brethren, the gospel which I preached to you, which also you received, in which also you stand, by which also you are saved, if you hold fast the word which I preached to you, unless you believed in vain. For I delivered to you as of first importance what I also received, that Christ died for our sins according to the Scriptures, and that He was buried, and that He was raised on the third day according to the Scriptures'*.

Christ died for our sins; that is the gospel. How then can

we be guilty? If we can save ourselves, we wouldn't need a saviour. Matthew 1:21 says it is Jesus who will save people from their sins. Isaiah 53:5 says Jesus was pierced for our trespasses, and was crushed for our iniquities. The chastisement for our well-being fell upon him, and by his scourging, we are healed. Verse 6 tells us that all of us like sheep have gone astray; each of us has turned his own way. But the Lord has caused the iniquity of us all to fall on him. Luke 2:11 says a saviour has come to the world who is Christ the Lord.

The enemy thinks of course that we haven't read our Bible, or that we don't understand it. We do because we have an anointing, and the anointing teaches us about all things, and it is true and not a lie (1 John 2:27). Satan is the lie. Our in-dwelling Spirit is the spirit of truth, and he guides us into all truth (John 16:13). We don't care for what the deceiver says about the Bible or its meaning. The Holy Spirit, the author of the Scripture, lives in us, and it is what he says that we listen to. Satan is a liar, deceiver and perverter, and he is looking for whom to deceive (1 Peter 5:8). The accuser will try his best to convince you of his lies. He will even use the Bible. Your knowledge of the Word of God is crucial to silencing the accuser. You need to know what the Word says the blood has done for you. You need to understand what salvation means.

Salvation

Salvation is by faith, not works. You cannot be effective against the accuser unless you fortify your mind with the word on salvation—that is what the helmet of salvation means. It protects the mind, the target of the enemy's lies.

The Bible says in Romans 1:16, *'For I am not ashamed of the gospel, for it is the power of God for salvation to everyone who believes'*. Verse 17 says in it the righteousness of God is revealed, a righteousness that is by faith from first to last, from the beginning to the end, springing from faith and leading to faith, just as it is written, the righteous will live by faith. This is the gospel with which you bruise the enemy. *'For by grace you have been saved through faith; and that not of yourselves, it is the gift of God; not as a result of works, so that no one may boast'* (Ephesians 2:8-9). God saved us, says 2 Timothy 1:9, not according to our works, but according to his own purpose and grace which was granted us in Christ Jesus from all eternity. He saved us, not on the basis of works which we have done in righteousness, but according to his mercy (Titus 3:5). I don't think it can be put any clearer than that.

We are not saved on the basis of any work that we have done in righteousness, or any work that we will do in righteousness, for having begun in faith, we cannot be perfected by works (Galatians 3:3-5). It is faith from the beginning to the end. Jesus was asked, *'What shall we do, so that we may work the works of God?'* His reply was, *'This is the work of God, that you believe in Him whom He has sent'* (John 6:28-29). Why is this important? Paul tells us that to the one who works, his wage is not reckoned as a favour or gift, but as what is due (Romans 4:4). But the Bible tells us that the only thing that is due to man is judgement, for all have sinned and fall short of the glory of God, and the wages of sin is death (Romans 3:23; 6:23). With God, the pass mark is one hundred percent. James 2:10 says whoever keeps the whole law and yet stumbles in one point, he has become guilty of all. The pass mark is one hundred percent. Be perfect, even as your heavenly Father is perfect (Matthew 5:48). Perfection is God's pass mark. Cursed is he who does not confirm the words of the law by doing them (Deuteronomy 27:26). To break one point of the law is to be cursed (Galatians 3:10).

It is therefore, absolutely impossible to be justified before God by works (Galatians 3:11). The purpose of the law is not justification. The law was meant by God to show us the need for a saviour (Galatians 3:11), and was to last only until the coming of Christ. Righteousness by works is humanly impossible; righteousness can only be by faith in Christ (Galatians 3:21-22). The purpose of the law was to bring us to Christ (Galatians 3:24), that we may be made right with God by faith in him. The good works we do cannot save us. Justification by works is out of the question. Paul says even the idea is the result of witchcraft (Galatians 3:1). It is a distortion of the gospel (Galatians 1:6-7), the work of the devil to lead people astray from the simplicity of faith in Christ (2 Corinthians 11:3-4). Once the enemy can get you to believe his version of the gospel, you have no defense against his accusations.

God says that we cannot live by the law (Ezekiel 20:25). Paul goes into much detail in Romans 7 to explain to us why this is so. The law is holy, righteous and good. It is the law of God. It reveals God's righteous standards. But we needed to be freed from it so that we can serve God and bear fruit for him (verse 4-6). We needed to be freed from the law because sin (Satan) was taking advantage of the law to bring guilt and condemnation (verse 9-11). Guilt and condemnation are the results of trying to live by the law. We were therefore made to die to the law through the body of Christ (verse 4). In Christ, condemnation is out of the question (John 3:18, Romans 8:1).

So we can see that it is impossible to earn righteousness. We cannot boast before God (Romans 4:2). Abraham believed God and it was reckoned to him as righteousness, for to the one who does not work, but believes in him who justifies the ungodly, his faith is reckoned as righteousness (verse 3-5). Salvation is by faith, pure and simple. It is the blood of Jesus plus nothing. By the works of the law, no flesh will be justified in God's sight,

> 'But now apart from the Law the righteousness of God has been manifested, being witnessed by the Law and the Prophets, even the righteousness of God through faith in Jesus Christ for all those who believe; for there is no distinction' (Romans 3:20-22).

We are all justified as a gift by his grace though the redemption which is in Christ Jesus, whom God displayed publicity as a propitiation in his blood through faith (verses 24-25).

The blood of Jesus is the answer to the enemy's accusations. Don't try anything else. Out knowledge of what the blood has done for us is absolutely essential. By the blood, we:

a. were redeemed (Ephesians 1:7, Colossians 1:14, Hebrews 9:12-15, 1 Peter 1:18-19, Revelations 1:5);
b. were purchased for God (Acts 20:28, Revelations 5:9);
c. were justified (Romans 5:9);
d. were released from the law (Hebrews 9:14);

e. were reconciled to God (Romans 5:10-11, Ephesians 2:13-16, 2 Corinthians 5:18);

f. have peace with God (Colossians 1:20, Romans 5:1);

g. we have access to God (Hebrews 10:19);

h. we were sanctified (Hebrews 13:12);

i. we were cleansed (1 John 1:7);

j. received propitiation (Romans 3:25);

k. we were saved (Romans 5:9).

In fact, the blood of Jesus is a metonym, that is, it represents everything Jesus has done for us. Jesus himself says we are to remember him by his blood (Luke 22:17-20, 1 Corinthians 11:23-25). It is the blood that we use to answer the accuser. In Zechariah 3, we see the accuser standing at Joshua, the high priest's right hand to accuse him. Joshua was wearing filthy garments, representing the sins of Israel. Their garments were filthy. They had sinned and were expelled from the Promised Land. But God is a God of grace and mercy, and he was inclined to restore the people to the land. But the accuser appeared to challenge the nation's entitlement to divine mercy. They were to keep on suffering in exile, the enemy demanded.

It is true that the people sinned, and it is true that we have sinned. And the enemy is constantly accusing. But in verse 2, God's answer to Satan is to get lost: 'The Lord rebuke you, Satan! Indeed the Lord who has chosen Jerusalem rebuke you'! Who will bring a charge against God's elect (Romans 8:33)? God is the one who justifies. If Satan has anything to say about you, let him go and say it to God. He will get a well—deserved 'get lost' reply from

God. Never listen to him or talk to him. Never answer his accusations. Your sins have been forgiven. Your filthy garments have been removed, and you are now clothed in the righteousness of Christ (Zechariah 3:4-5). Your robes have been cleansed in the blood of the lamb (Revelations 7:14).

The accuser can accuse from now till kingdom comes; that is his own business. We are not wearing the robes of our own efforts as in Matthew 22:11-13; we are clothed with the robes of the finished work of Jesus Christ. God says that Joshua and his friends are a symbol of what Christ, the branch, has done for us (Zechariah 3:8). They are a symbol of our Lord's vicarious work of atonement on our behalf, and all that he accomplished for us on the cross. That is the answer to the accuser. He is a liar. He does not stand in the truth, and his accusations are not worth our attention. We have been rescued from the fire (Zechariah 3:2). A born again Christian is a new creation (2 Corinthians 5:17). We are accepted (Romans 15:7); we are secure (Romans 8:38-39); we are blessed (Ephesians 1:3); we are free from guilt and condemnation (Romans 8:1, John 3:18). God does not condemn Jesus. We are in Christ, so God doesn't condemn us. He accepts us just as he accepts Jesus as his Son (John 1:12, Romans 8:14-16, Galatians 4:4-7). When God looks at us, he sees Christ. The enemy's accusations are meant to produce fear, but the Bible tells us that we are safe and secure in Christ. We have nothing to fear—not failure, not inadequacies and certainly not Satan.

Pray:

I am accepted in the beloved. I am safe and secure in Christ. The Lord rebuke the accuser, in Jesus' name. Amen.

The Murderer

SEVEN

Satan is a murderer. God himself tells us this in John 8:44. He was a murderer from the beginning. He comes only to steal and kill and destroy. He has been murdering since the beginning and he still murdering today. He lied to Eve that she would not die, but she died. Genesis 5 tells us all the generations died—all the work of the murderer. Today, he is still carrying on his evil and murderous work—through wars, abortion, suicide, murders, disease, etc. He is the architect of all evil, wickedness and ungodliness. In God is life (John 1:4), and Satan hates everything of God. He works through death, he loves death, and he will end up with death in the lake of fire (Revelations 20:10). He is a beast who delights in murdering the innocent. Everyone who as ever killed has only been a puppet of the real murderer, who is behind the scene. 1 John 3:8 tells us that the devil is the architect of all wickedness, perversity and evil. He has been sinning from the beginning, and Jesus came to destroy his work.

Cain and Abel

When Cain murdered his brother, Abel, he was only showing his pedigree (John 3:12). He was showing that he was of the evil one. The enemy seeks to murder every righteous person. In Genesis 4, we see the result of false religion, one of the murderous weapons of the enemy. Abel (true faith) heard from God (Hebrews 11:4), brought an offering acceptable to the Lord by making the required blood sacrifice, and he obtained the testimony that he was righteous. Cain (false religion), acting on presumption, brought an offering of the fruit of the curse ground to the Lord, which was unacceptable to God, and he was rejected. False religion—coming to the Lord except by the blood of the Lamb, isn't acceptable to God.

False religions are satanic inventions to perpetrate murder. The followers of those religions who themselves do not commit acts of murder end up lost anyway. Satan is a murderer. But here in Genesis 4, we see Cain, of the devil, following the thoughts planted by the devil. Cain didn't hear from God, but followed his own thoughts— planted by the devil. The devil is the thought-caster. The thoughts of God are contained in his Word, and anything outside of it is of the devil—but the enemy deceives people into thinking they are their own thoughts. God says to follow one's thoughts is like witchcraft, divination and idolatry (1 Samuel 15:23). To follow one's thoughts is to reject the thoughts of the Lord; it is to heed the voice of the enemy. Someone has said that when God shattered Satan on the cross, the only thing he left Satan was his voice—and the murderer is still speaking evil today.

To follow any other creed apart from Christianity is to

end up rejected by God and estranged from him, his righteousness, peace and joy (Romans 14:17). When there is no peace and joy, there is hatred, anger, depression, and murder (Genesis 4:5-8, Matthew 5:21-22, 1 John 3:15). Cain was rejected by God, since he was following the enemy's thoughts. To follow the Lord is to have peace, joy and hope (Genesis 4:7, Romans 15:13). To follow the devil is to have none of these things. The result of following the devil is to be devoured by the beast (Genesis 4:7). Cain murdered his brother (verse 8) as many of the devil's children are doing today. 'Am I my brother's keeper?' he asked the Lord (verse 9). Cain's relatives are still asking the same question today. 'Is it our job to see to the well-being of our neighbours? Isn't it every man for himself, and the devil catch the hindmost?' they ask.

We are our neighbour's keeper. Jesus says our neighbours aren't just our friends, relatives, townspeople, race or fellow nationals. Jesus says our neighbour is anyone in need of our help or assistance (Luke 10:29-37). We are our neighbours' keepers. But the devil, vociferous as he is, only speaks foul nonsense—and many people believe him. Cain believed Satan and murdered his brother, for which God cursed him, as he cursed Satan in Genesis 3:14. The voice of Abel's blood is crying out, and the blood of every victim of the devil is crying out against him and the murderers of this world today. Satan is a vagabond (Job 1:7), and Cain became a vagabond (Genesis 4:14). Every murderer becomes a partaker of the vagabond spirit, for there is no peace for the wicked. They are like the troubled sea, they cannot rest (Isaiah 57:20-12).

Jesus says the world will hate believers (John 15:19)

and persecute them (verse 20). Hatred and persecution are expressions of the spirit of murder (1 John 3:15, Matthew 5:21-22). Satan hates believers, and his followers partake of this hatred. Many saints have been martyred by people under the direct control of the murderer himself. Many saints are still being persecuted today all over the world. Let us remember them in our prayers. Satan is a murderer. He seeks to use murder to achieve his aims on earth, but he will never succeed. He produced a race of crazy half-demons on earth to spread murder and violence across the earth, and thwart the coming of the Messiah (Genesis 6:4-11). He failed of course. God destroyed the race of half-demons in the flood and imprisoned the evil spirits that produced them (Jude 6).

Satan manipulates nations (Revelations 12:9; 19:19; 20:38), deceiving them to engage in wars, so that he could murder millions. In the First World War, twenty million people lost their lives. Fifty-five million were killed in the Second World War, including six million Jews—the ancient targets of Satan's hatred and murder (Revelations 12:4, 13 and 15). Millions have been killed in subsequent wars, and the numbers are rising. There are wars going on all over the world today—with deceit as the basis. Just what the enemy wants. The enemy though powerless, is a master of deceit. He doesn't play by any rules. He is a crafty, subtle deceiver; he does not care what the issue is by which a person is deceived so long as they are deceived.

He is a murderer. He attacks life and the capacity of life. He seeks to murder all—believers, unbelievers, Israel, the Church, nations, generations, individuals, etc. He desires to murder every one that threatens his evil agenda, especially the Church-age believer (2 Corinthians 2:11; 11:3, Ephesians 6:10-12, James 4:6-10, 1 Peter 5:6-9). He deceives multitudes into carrying out his plans for him, thus appearing to be powerful. The real truth about Satan's power is that he has none. Deception is evidence of powerlessness. His real agenda is to be worshipped as God, and he is a schemer. He wants revenge for being humiliated and thrown down from heaven. He wants to make life a misery for everyone, and chief of all, he wants to be like God! He also has his schemes—foolish schemes (praise God). He wasn't content with guarding God's throne. He wants to sit on it. Extreme pride (Job 41:34) seeks dominance. He failed in heaven, so he is trying to succeed on earth, with murder, threats and fear as his tools.

The Three Hebrew Children

In Daniel 3, we see the devil unveiled. Nebuchadnezzar, a type of satanic pride, made a golden image. God had revealed to him in Daniel 2 that he was to be the head of gold. But pride had to be dominant. Instead of just being the head of gold, he wanted to be everything. So he made a statue of gold from head to toe, challenging God's will and seeking to perpetuate his kingdom. No doubt Satan was inspiring him. Daniel 3:1 tells us the statue was ninety feet high, so you couldn't miss it: big ego, big pride, big statue. He set it up in the plain of Dura (circle), so that the statue would be the centre of attention, and would be seen by all and sundry. He then summoned all the rulers to the dedication of the image. Compare the titles in verses 2 and 3 with those in Ephesians 1:21 and 6:12 and you will see that we are seeing the devil in operation here. And he is still doing the same today. He is still getting the whole world to listen to his lies and watch his images (movies). The world media is spreading his message and billions are hearing them. Leaders from every walk of life were invited, not the ordinary folks. Leaders are in control of the machinery that Satan needs to carry out his evil work. A Christian politician once said that when politicians get into government, Satan is waiting for them. We see it here. Satan can get one Hitler to murder fifty-five million people, you see.

The statue was made of gold, ninety feet high and set in the middle of Dura with the sun blazing overhead. The leaders could not but be impressed. Satan is a schemer. Having got the leaders, he then commanded them and everyone else to do as he says (verse 4)—peoples, nations and men of every language. The enemy commands and he shouts (verse 4). He thinks shouting will bring about universal obedience to his evil commands. Let him shout as long as he likes. He has threatened to shout down God and his kingdom, and God has left him his voice to show him what a fool he is. God is wiser than Satan. He has nothing and no one to fear. He usually works by letting fools prove their folly. He could have taken away Satan's voice when he took away his powers, but he left him his voice. Satan needs to prove his folly. The Bible says when a fool is silent, no one knows he is a fool (Proverbs 17:28). So when God let Satan talk, he wasn't doing Satan any favours at all. He was only allowing him to show his folly to everyone. So let him shout on. In verse 4, he shouted his evil command at all the people, without exception. There was no opt-out clause. Do as I say or die, he threatened. He wants the whole world, all peoples, nations and languages, but we know what he is going to get—a roasting. He commanded everyone. He loves no one. All those demons and witches serving him are likewise targets of his evil—ask ex-witches, they will tell you.

He then commanded music to be played (verse 6). He is still using music to get people to worship him today. Rock-and-roll, heavy metal, etc. are all tools in the enemy's hands. Here we see the link between worship and music. Today, rock stars and pop idols are objects of worship and they all have an image, usually crafted by some agency and costing huge sums of money. Image is very important in the music industry. Today, it is all about sex. Good music died. Sex is the god of the age. The sex industry isn't limited to prostitutes anymore. It has become a leading industry. Sex is used to sell records, cars, even washing powder. Politicians can control themselves when it comes to silver, but Satan gets them with sex.

Whoever does not fall down and worship will immediately be thrown into a blazing furnace (verse 6). The bully threatens death by roasting (his own destiny). He always threatens—that's one way to identity him. He is a bully, and he expects you to act on his lies immediately. Noise and hurry are his favourite schemes. But the thief isn't going to get his way—never. God's heroes don't bow to threats and fear. It is fear that must bow. We have been called to be fearless—to be a hero means to be above fear. Verse 8-12 tells us that some disreputable people—demon-possessed astrologers and diviners, enemies of God deserving death themselves (Exodus 22:18, Leviticus 19:26,31; 20:6,27, Deuteronomy 18:10-14) came forward with accusations against God's heroes, people who dare to love God and worship him rather than the lunatic Satan. It is not our job to bow to the thief. He is entitled only to our contempt. So Nebuchadnezzar, in satanic rage and anger (Revelations 12:12), gave orders for Shadrach, Meshach and Abednego to be brought before him (Daniel 3:13). He reissued his commands and threats, with fear as the lever, but God's heroes can't be intimidated (verse 14-18). Satan has no power. He is a defeated foe. The heroes' reply was simple, 'There is nothing to talk about.' We have nothing to discuss with Satan. God has called us to evangelize, not analyse. If God wants us here—and he does—he will keep us. He has promised to do so. We are not going to bow to any foul spirit.

God delivered his heroes from the fire (Isaiah 43:1-4), and Satan's men ended up being roasted (Daniel 3:22), and there was nothing that Satan could do to help them (but he doesn't really care—verse 19-30). That God's people will burn is a lie. It is Satan and those who obey him that will burn. The liar, being a perverse spirit, likes to reverse the truth. Beware of him. The secret of lying is to make it sound convincing, but a lie has no power unless it is believed. As long as you don't believe his lies, Satan can huff and puff, shout and scream as long as he likes. He cannot control your choices and he cannot make you do anything. You are immune. A roaring lion (1 Peter 5:8) is a bluffing lion. The roar is meant to paralyse with fear so that it becomes easier for the thief to strike. If you don't freeze when he growls, there is nothing he can do to you. It is those who allow themselves to be paralysed by fear that the enemy devours.

Pray:

I refuse fear, in Jesus' name. Satan has no power over me. Amen.

Satan is a murderer. Jesus tells us in Matthew 23:29-35 that the devil and his followers are guilty of all the righteous blood shed on earth. The murderer is still at work today, and the book of Revelations tells us of the murders that the beast is still going to perpetrate on earth. Let us resist the murderer in the name of Jesus.

Pray:

In the name of Jesus, I declare that no weapon fashioned against me shall prosper. God is my mighty rock and I am safe in him. Amen.

Our Weapons

EIGHT

The weapons of our warfare are not weapons of this world (2 Corinthians 10:4), but are mighty through God. They have divine power to demolish, overthrow and destroy every stronghold of evil. We do not use human weapons against the enemy. Physical weapons cannot frustrate the enemy's plans to turn this world into a stronghold of evil and rebellion. The God of all grace has mercifully supplied us with mighty weapons to frustrate the evil architect of iniquity, wickedness and ungodliness in our life and in our world.

Carnal Weapons

What are the weapons of the flesh? Paul in Ephesians 4:17-32 and Colossians 3:5-11 tells us what these are. The world fights with these weapons and they perish with them. They are weapons of the devil and futility. They are weapons of ignorance and darkness. They have no place in the life of a believer. The world will deceive and be deceived. The world uses anger as a weapon of intimidation and control. They rage, fume and scream like their master to get their own way. The world will steal as they deem necessary. Evil speaking, slander and accusation are common tools of advancement in the world. Idolatry, witchcraft and spiritism are seen as normal. Psychic hotlines are the order of the day. New-age lies are openly promoted. All sort of evil practices are resorted to as means of 'succeeding' in life.

Factionalism, division and party spirit are used to achieve ambitions (1 Corinthians 3:3). Satanic wisdom is being sought and used by ignorant people, to their own detriment (James 3:14-16). The arm of the flesh is what many rely on (Jeremiah 17:5). Trust is placed in princes and chariots (Psalms 20:7-8; 146:3). Some live according to their own thoughts (Psalm 146:4, 1 Corinthians 1:19-20; 2:6; 3:18-20). God is not against human knowledge; we all need knowledge. It is human wisdom (which is satanic wisdom) that God forbids. And these are the weapons that the world lives by—and perishes by. Many make money their fortresses, while others rely on legalism, religion, nationality, family, race, personality and human efforts—all dung, according to Paul in Philippians 3:3-11. These are the weapons of the flesh; they are not our weapons.

Spiritual Weapons

We fight the enemy primarily with spiritual weapons. The Scripture contains a plethora of spiritual weapons for the warfare of the believer. These weapons are designed to frustrate the enemy as he tries to impose his evil will on our will, and as he tries to impose evil emotions, behaviours or circumstances on us that we would not otherwise want. They are our armour against satanic coercion, intimidation, manipulation domination and control. They were given to us by God to prevent Satan from projecting his evil successfully into out life and circumstances. Satan is the deadliest force on earth today as far as his agenda is concerned. Our job is to use our mighty weapons to thwart his plans. Satan is deadly if allowed to operate unchecked. The weapons of our warfare are meant to stop the enemy from encroaching on our capacity for life and godliness. So these weapons are of great importance to our total well-being. The Bible says the enemy demands that we lie down that he may walk over us (Isaiah 51:23). Well, we are not going to lie down. Not for a fool like Satan and not for anybody else. We are here to deal with him, not to surrender to him. That is why we have our weapons.

The Blood of Jesus

The first of these weapons is the Blood of Jesus. We saw in chapter six that the Blood of Jesus is at the centre of everything Jesus accomplished for us on the cross—it symbolizes the power of the cross that broke Satan's back. The Blood stands for Jesus' substitutionary work of atonement on our behalf. It is at the centre of our redemption. It stands for the complete and finished work of the cross. It is the Blood of our redemption, justification, sanctification, release, purchase, reconciliation, peace, access, cleansing, propitiation and salvation. It is our most powerful weapon against the thief (Revelations 12:22).

Pray:

By the power of the Blood of Jesus, I trample over Satan, his demons and agents, in Jesus' name. Amen.

The Name of Jesus

Everything must bow at the Name of Jesus (Philippians 2:10). The Bible does not say that every knee WILL bow. It says every knee MUST bow. Isaiah 45:23, looking forward to the cross, says every knee will bow. Philippians 2:10, looking back to the cross, now declares that every knee must bow. They are not going to bow at some future time. They must bow now. Make the enemy bow in your life at the Name of Jesus. Jesus tells us to pray in his Name (John 14:12-14; 16:23-26). His Name is what we are to use to do the greater works that he wants us to do. The Name of Jesus is a mighty fortress against the enemy. Through the Name of Jesus, we cut off and extinguish our enemies (Psalm 118:10-12). Satan has no defense against that Name (Acts 3:16).

Pray:

In the mighty Name of Jesus, I cut off all those evil spirits warring against my life. Amen.

Praise and Worship

Praise and worship are mighty weapons against the enemy. The Bible tells us to worship God. It doesn't however say that God is looking for worship. He is looking for worshippers (John 4:23). It is the thief that is looking for worship. God is looking for worshippers, and we are his worshippers. We worship God because he is worthy of all glory, honour and praise. Satan is not worthy of our worship. He is worthy of contempt, condemnation and destruction—and that is what he will get. When we worship God as the Bible says, we are in fact executing judgement on the enemy (Psalm 149:6-9). We are heaping the shame due to Satan on him, and hurting his pride, the main motivation for his evil deeds. We are denying him of what he wants most, to which he is not entitled. When we worship God, we are upholding the truth—that God is worthy. Healings, deliverances, blessings, etc. come to us from the God of grace as we worship him. We don't worship him for these things. We worship him because he is worthy. But in his goodness, he blesses us as we praise him because God is a giver and he is a good God.

Praise is a mighty weapon against the enemy. In Genesis, 43:8, Judah (praise) was the guarantor of Benjamin's well-being. Praising God guarantees us good. Only good comes to us when we worship God. In God's presence, there is fullness of joy, and at his right hand, there are pleasures forever (Psalm 16:11). In Genesis 46:28, we see Joseph sending Judah (praise) ahead of him to meet Joseph and get directions to Goshen. The Bible tells us in Psalm 100:4 to enter the gates of the Lord with thanksgiving and enter his courts with praise. As we come into the presence of the Lord, praise is the first thing due to him. If we were to behold him now face-to-face, we would know that it is so. The Lord is an awesome God. He is worthy of praise and the right thing as we approach him is to send our praises first. Let us praise

God today (Psalm 103:1-5). As we praise him, the enemy is humiliated.

Pray:

I worship you, O God of heaven and earth. You are worthy of all my praise. In Jesus' name. Amen.

The Full Armour

We are an army at war. We are engaged in a face-to-face, hand-to-hand conflict to the finish with forces of evil, says Ephesians 6:12. Christianity is not a Sunday school picnic. We need to be continually empowered by God to disgrace the adversary. A face-to-face, hand-to-hand conflict demands head-to-toe protection. God supplies us with the armour, but it is our job to use it against the host of evil forces opposing us. Ephesians 6:10 tells us to be strong in the Lord and in the power of his might. Verse 11 says we are to put on the full armour of God that we may be able to stand firm against the enemy—resisting him, holding our position and offering no surrender to the enemy of righteousness as he fights to defeat the Church of God and turn us away from Christ and back to sin. When we become God's children, we inherit God's enemies, and Satan is chief among them. We are told to stand firm against him three times (verse 11, 13, 14; see also James 4:7, 1 Peter 5:8-9). The panoply we have been given against his tricks, schemes, stratagems, wiles and devices are:

a. Belt of Truth

Paul was chained to a Roman soldier when he wrote Ephesians, and the soldier's armour must have provided him the idea of the panoply. The order in which a soldier would put on the pieces of his armour is the same as the order of the pieces in Ephesians 6:14-17. First the belt is tightened around the waist to indicate preparedness for action (verse 14, 1 Peter 1:13). A slackened belt meant 'off duty'. The belt holds together the tunic and it holds other pieces of the armour in place such as the breastplate and the sheath for the sword. It is the foundational piece and for the Christian, the belt means truth. Truth is revealed in the Word of God (Ephesians 1:13, Colossians 1:5). The Word is our weapon against the father of lies (John 8:44). When he attacks us, we must stand firm in the truth of the Word of God.

b. Breastplate of Righteousness

Next is the breastplate of righteousness (verse 14). The breastplate protects the vital organs of the body. It covers the body from the neck to the thighs. Often a back piece was worn as well. We are not to seek protection in any work of our own but only in what Christ has done for us. We have been made the righteousness of God in him (2 Corinthians 5:21). To seek to use our own efforts is to be vulnerable, defeated and disgraced by the accuser.

c. Shoes of the Gospel of Peace

Next, the soldier puts on his strong army boots which ensure a good grip (verse 15). Not only were the feet well protected, the soldier could undertake long marches at great speed over rough terrain. He could also dig in and hold his ground when in hand-to-hand combat. For the believer, this means that we can stand firm in battle, with peace, because we know that we have been reconciled to God (Ephesians 2:17).

d. Shield of Faith

Next, the soldier takes his shield for full protection (verse 16). As total reliance on and trust in God, his faithfulness, character, power, presence, and Word, faith is the ultimate weapon of all. Jesus raised faith to the first place. Be it unto you according to your faith, he says in Matthew 9:29. Faith is our greatest weapon. Faith puts God between us and the enemy. It is the substance of what we hope for, the evidence of what we do not see. By it we know who, when, where, why and how. Faith is the legal tender in God's economy. It is perhaps the most powerful element on earth. It pleases God, and it moves mountains. It repels the enemy. It is a great weapon indeed. It strengthens the soul and lightens the spirit. It is our foremost weapon. Jesus commended it; Satan has no answer to it. Our hearts are purified by it; we are established in the Christian life by it. We are comforted by it, and we live by it. We are made right with God by it, and we have peace by it. We have access to God by it, and we stand by it. We eat our food by it, and we walk by it. We are sanctified by it, and we are blessed by it. We receive the Holy Spirit by it; we receive the promises by it. We are saved by it, and Christ's presence dwells in our heart by it. We have joy by it, and we are kept by it. We fight by it, and we quench Satan's missiles by it. Faith is the key principle of the Christian life. All things are possible to it, and the enemy is after it.

Nothing that the enemy throws at us can withstand faith (Ephesians 6:16). Faith quenches the diabolical missiles of the wicked one—be they temptations, despair, lust, doubt, discouragement, wrath, problems, criticism, vengeance, trials or persecution. Faith counteracts them all.

e. Helmet of Salvation

Next is the helmet (verse 17a). It protects the soldier's head. No sword could pierce a good helmet. The helmet of present assurance of a given and accomplished salvation, protects our mind from all attacks of the evil one—empty, futile, vain and evil thoughts, doubt, etc. It gives us boldness and confidence against the enemy.

f. The Sword of the Spirit

The final piece of the soldier's armour is the sword (verse 176), the only offensive weapon mentioned. It refers to the short sword used in close combat. The Christian's sword is provided by the Spirit. The Spirit supplies us with the words to use to drive Satan away (Matthew 4:1-11), as well as making them effective (John 6:63) and penetrating (Hebrews 4:12).

Pray:

I take up the full armour of God, in Jesus' name. Amen.

Prayer

The full armour supplied in Ephesians 6:14-17 is to be worn in connection with prayer. Prayer is our inter-continental ballistic missile. It gets anyone, anywhere, anytime. Satan hates a praying Christian. When you are praying, you are calling unto God for help and Satan knows he is in trouble. He will even try to distract you. Ephesians 6:18 says we should pray at all times with all prayer and petition in the Spirit. Jesus says we ought to pray at all times and not lose heart (Luke 18:1; 6:12). 1 Thessalonians 5:17 says we should pray without ceasing. Praying in the Spirit, with all kinds of prayer—intercession, decree, supplication, thanksgiving, confession and adoration—will ensure constant victory for us as we take up our armour against the enemy. We need to pray as well as know the Scriptures. To know the Scriptures without praying is only tickling the mind. To pray without knowing the Word is to pray ineffectively. Spiritual understanding combined with alert and persistent prayerfulness under the Spirit's guidance is a deadly cocktail to the enemy. Prayer can be combined with fasting to bring greater force to bear on the enemy (Isaiah 58:6, Matthew 17:21).

Pray:

In the name of Jesus, I decree God's will, blessing and breakthrough in my life. I decree health, success, restoration, prosperity, deliverance, divine protection and peace. I decree total victory over the enemy. Amen.

Silence

Silence is a powerful weapon. Its importance has been overlooked by modern man. Modern man has become attuned to noise. The cacophony of noises in the modern world has robbed people of the inner culture of quietness and silence. The Bible plainly tells us that in quietness and silence is our strength (Isaiah 7:4; 30:15). The effect of righteousness is quietness, and the final outworking of faith is stillness. God commands us continually to be still and to cultivate quietness (Exodus 14:14, Psalm 4:4; 37:7). We need quietness to hear from God (1 Samuel 9:27). We need quietness to know what the Lord wants us to know (Psalm 46:10). You see, Satan is a lunatic in every sense of the word. Why should we make ourselves like him? Lunatics can't rest or be still. We have been called to peace and quietness. When Satan barks, we don't bark in return. We just ignore him and be quiet. We maintain our strength that way. Satan wants to wear you out, and inward plus outward chattering are some of his tools in this regard. He hates people being quiet. If you try to be quiet, he will send one of his demons to come and stir you up and agitate you.

Silence keeps us strong and fresh. People of faith are people of silence. People of fear are people of overwork, noise and busyness. To be quiet is to trust God. Lack of silence is abnormal, and this world has become just that. Great men and women are formed in the quiet repose of the heart, not in the busyness, noise, hurry and heat of the rush hour. Useless activities are considered better than the practice of silence. We Christians sometimes feel that if we are not doing something, we are not pleasing God. This is certainly not true. Overwork is not a virtue. It is a vice. Silence generates inner strength to accomplish our work, while noise depletes our energy. A person who cannot be still is a driven person. Many people know that they are driven, but they just can't stop. They need deliverance.

Too much talk, too much action scatters our energy and often leaves us exhausted and weary.

Many modern-day illnesses have their root in over-work, hurry and noise. We are not meant to function that way. The Bible says success does not depend on the man who wills or the man who runs, but on God who has mercy (Romans 9:16). Ecclesiastes 9:11 says the race is not to the swift. Therefore, achievement is not always the result of excessive busyness. God can't bless strife. Rush may get temporary results, but stillness wins lasting prizes. Quietness is a powerful weapon against the enemy. It is evidence of self-control and power. Modern Christians have generally regarded silence as something that belongs to medieval monasticism. Silence however is needed by people of every age. God works in the silence, not in the commotion. Elijah heard God in a still small voice—not in the wind, earthquake of fire (1 Kings 19:11-12). It is in the silence of the night that much of nature's work in done (Mark 4:26-29). How the crop grows, the farmer does not know. The soil produces crops by itself, verse 28 says.

Silence is of great value to us. Our success depends on knowing how to be still and trust God to do what he alone can do. We have our part to play of course, but success only comes from God (1 Corinthians 3:6). It is the blessing of the Lord that brings success in life (Proverbs 10:22), and he only blesses us when we trust him enough to rest in him (Psalm 37:3-7). Without quietness, the enemy can harass us. There isn't much he can do when we are still except to bark on toothlessly. Let us leave needless dialogue, idle talk and inward chatter alone. Let us cultivate quietness today.

Pray:

In the name of Jesus, I let go and let God. Amen.

Miscellaneous Weapons

Many other weapons are available to us. We shall discover them as we search the Scriptures. Love is a powerful weapon (Romans 12:9; 13:8-10, 1 Corinthians 13, Colossians 3:14). We all need hope. In fact, hope is the reason for faith. We must never allow the enemy to steal our hope (Romans 12:12; 15:13). The joy of the Lord is our strength (Nehemiah 8:10). We need joy and laughter to have a good life (Romans 15:13). Rest and leisure are also necessary for a balanced life. We are not just here to fight. Patience is necessary to win every battle. Likewise, persistence is a great weapon. The enemy won't give up. Neither should we. Boldness is a necessary quality in believers (Proverbs 28:1). The anointing of the Holy Spirit is a mighty resource (Acts 1:8, Romans 15:13). It is the anointing that destroys the yoke (Isaiah 10:27). The Spirit is our continual strengthener, teacher, helper, comforter and guide (John 14:16; 15:26; 16:13-14). The Bible says we are to be continually filled with the Spirit (Ephesians 5:18). The Bible mentions many other weapons which you may use against the enemy, such as God's thunder, lightening, earthquake, fire, sword, woe, pestilence, deluge and the curse of the Lord against satanic forces. Let us bombard the enemy continually in Jesus' name.

Pray:

In the name of Jesus, I send the sword of the Lord against every evil spirit fighting against me. Amen.

Appendix

SPIRITUAL WARFARE VERSES

Matthew 16:18-19

Luke 10:18-19

Luke 11:22

John 12:31

Romans 7:6

Romans 8:15

Romans 8:31

Romans 8:33

Romans 8:37

1 Corinthians 15:57

2 Corinthians 2:14

2 Corinthians 5:21

2 Corinthians 10:4-5

Galatians 3:13

Ephesians 6:11

Colossians 2:15

1 Timothy 1:18

2 Timothy 2:4

Hebrews 2:14-15

James 4:7

1 Peter 5:8-9

1 John 3:8

1 John 4:4

1 John 5:4

Revelations 2:11

Revelations 20:10

CPSIA information can be obtained at www.ICGtesting.com
Printed in the USA
BVOW04s2221140813

328731BV00001B/58/A